Dedications

Adele

High School Sweetheart; Ministry Partner;
Administrative Assistant; Best Friend; Dearly Loved Wife;
My Greatest Human Example of Grace, Mercy, and Love.

Axel and Kaylee

I love you. Jesus loves you.
I pray you will grow up to love Him
and His Bride.

To Love and To Cherish From This Day Forward
...A Portrait of a Healthy Church

Randy Millwood

simplymillwood

Mark: Welcome to BCMV. I am so glad you are here! I look forward to serving the LORD by serving His Bride with you!

Randy

Copyright © 2010 by Randy Millwood

ISBN-13: 978-1475192155
ISBN-10: 1475192150

All rights reserved. No part of this book may be used or reproduced in any manner whatsoever without written permission, except in the case of brief quotations embodied in critical articles or reviews.

Printed in the United States of America

Scripture quotations marked NLT are taken from the *Holy Bible*, New Living Translation, copyright 1996, 2004. Used by permission of Tyndale House Publishers, Inc., Carol Stream, Illinois 60188. All rights reserved.

Scripture taken from *The Message* (MSG), copyright 1993, 1994, 1995, 1996, 2000, 2001, 2002. Used by permission of NavPress Publishing Group.

Scripture taken from the Holy Bible, New International Version®, (NIV) Copyright © 1973, 1978, 1984, Biblica. Used by permission of Zondervan. All rights reserved.

Scripture taken from the New Century Version (NCV). Copyright © 2005 by Thomas Nelson, Inc. Used by permission. All rights reserved.

Good News Translation® (Today's English Version, Second Edition) Copyright © 1992 American Bible Society. All rights reserved.

Cover Photo: © Artist/Designer: Samantha Raynor

ACKNOWLEDGEMENTS

A purebred or pedigreed dog is one with a pure lineage. A crossbred is a pup from two purebreds (for example a Peekapoo or a Goldendoodle). But, if the breeds are generations removed from pure or crossbred, they are known as mixed breeds, or a loveable *mutt*. *That's me* (at least the *mutt* part).

I am, in broad, irreversible ways, the consequence or result of all the books, blogs, tweets, or articles I've read... of all the conference speakers I've heard…of all the conversations I've been a part of…of all of the classes I've attended. It would be impossible to thank all of those people. But I can and do thank God for all of them.

However, there are a few people I simply must identify and say *thanks* to:

Mom and Dad – for laying foundations to last a lifetime

Ken, Fred and Bill – for trusting, investing, and entrusting

Ferris – for not letting me quit, ever

Chuck – for challenging me to go someplace I may never have gone

Jeanine and Bob – for encouragement and research help

John, Brian and David – for helping me ask questions and keeping me objective (and John, thanks for letting me use the *umbrella* image)

David, Mel and Bob – for giving me time to write

D J, David, Reggie, Ferris, Daryl, Will, Eddie, and Jason – for reading and offering words of encouragement

David – for being a bold risk-taker and constant encourager

Sam – for the beauty of design, the irony of images, and the cheer of color; genius

Jason – for *loving* technology, but loving God and people *more*

Josh – for reading *every* page, challenging *every* idea, encouraging and offering clear suggestions and directions… this would not be, without you

Caleb – for always asking the practical questions

Elena – for an artful eye and for helping prepare and host all of the web-based support for this project

Adele – for showing me, day in and day out, what the Christ-life should look like; for traveling this journey with me, in spite of the wandering times; for asking critical questions; for reviewing and responding; for being my best friend; for more than words or space allow

Jesus – for not giving up *on* me while giving up so much *for* me

WHAT OTHERS ARE SAYING

Leaders need to make sure they are working on the right questions. Answering the wrong questions precisely right still won't matter! Randy Millwood gives church leaders a better set of questions to work on than the ones consuming so many. Don't read this book if you want to figure out how to do church better; by all means read it if you want to BE church better.

Reggie McNeal
Author of <i>Missional Renaissance: Changing The Scorecard for the Church</i>
Missional Leadership Specialist
Leadership Network
leadnet.org/reggiemcneal

Possibly never before in the history of the Church is such a book needed to encourage followers of Jesus to love the Bride of Christ, like He loves her. It is easy to become disillusioned and disenchanted with the institutional church. Randy Millwood skillfully and poetically examines the characteristics of a healthy Bride and inspires Christian leaders to equip the Church to live out her passion for Christ in a skeptical world. This book offers real hope for those desiring to follow the "Way" of Jesus and experience real community.

Daryl Eldridge
President
Rockbridge Seminary

I know Randy Millwood. He is the real deal. He lives what he writes. In *To Love and to Cherish from This Day Forward*, Randy calls on the church to be the real deal, to understand clearly what the writers of the New Testament wrote and practiced, and to live and make disciples accordingly. This is a must read for those who are serious about growing a healthy, disciple-making church.

David Lee
Executive Director
Baptist Convention of Maryland/Delaware

Randy Millwood offers a powerful, personal contribution to missional writings as he provides sound theological insights cradled in stories of God's transforming work in people, churches and the world. A tool for those in pulpits, pews and leadership in the world as the church at work in the world! Thanks Randy!

Edward Hammett
Author of *Spiritual Leadership in a Secular Age*
Partner with The Columbia Partnership
www.thecolumbiapartnership.org

Here comes the Bride! In *To Love and To Cherish from This Day Forward*, Randy Millwood has provided an enjoyable and winsome look at the Bride of Christ, the church. Using the analogy of 1st century Jewish marriage practices to inform the modern reader, he offers a helpful critique to those of us within the Body of Christ, calling her to be about healthy disciple-making by focusing on the process rather than the results. Millwood reminds Christ-followers to live out the wonder of their relationship with the Bridegroom before the eyes of the world.

David Jackson
Church Multiplication Strategist, BCMD
Author of *PlantLIFE: Principles and Practices of Church Planting*

Casual, fresh, and insightful, a great combination for a book on such vital subject areas as church health and making more disciples. Randy has a unique way of communicating significant insights intertwined with everyday stories. There are truths about our life in Christ and His church that you don't want to miss. If you are wondering what it means to be a church in the midst of all the spiritual confusion, read this book. It might just give you some new perspectives and pieces of the mosaic puzzle you have been missing.

Will McRaney
Director of Evangelism Strategy
Florida Baptist Convention
Author of *The Art of Personal Evangelism*

Among the mentors who have most shaped my understanding of "church" and "mission" and "discipling" and "equipping," Randy is at the top of the list. This is his heart and wisdom shared for our benefit and ultimately for the benefit of those to whom we will live sent in our daily lives. A very important book for the church of America to read and to apply.

Jason Dukes
Pastor, Westpoint Church
Author of *Live Sent: you are a letter*
www.LiveSent.com

FOREWORD

I have been the recipient of blessings through a local church ever since I was taken there while in my mother's womb. In the church environment I yielded my life to Jesus as Savior, grew as a disciple, and answered God's call to preach. By God's grace, I served several churches as pastor. For twenty years I taught in a seminary, seeking to equip ministers to serve local churches.

Despite that journey and my biblical and theological studies, too often I have thought of church in terms of organization, policies and procedures, programs, and agendas. Too easily the wonder of the church as God's redeemed people "from every nation, tribe, people and language" (Rev. 7:9) has eluded me.

Paul described the church as a new humanity (Eph. 2:15). He taught that all believers have been brought together to live in peace with God and in harmonious fellowship with one another through the blood of Jesus. The church is God's new creation.

Moreover, this unique creation is designed and destined to display God's multi-faceted wisdom "to the rulers and the authorities in the heavenly *places*" (Eph. 3:10 NASB). God's praise and glory are to be declared in and by the church.

Have you ever stood in awe of some aspect of God's first creation, such as the Grand Canyon, and exclaimed, "How could anyone see the splendor of this place and not believe in God?" Well, it is God's intention that the world look at God's second creation, the church, and be led to acknowledge His wisdom and immeasurable grace.

Considering God's intention leads to my concern that local expressions of Christ's body are not always fulfilling that purpose. The unhealthy state of many local fellowships prevents persons from looking at them and marveling at God's wisdom and grace.

My former student, my friend, and my colleague in ministry, Randy Millwood, has had a growing concern across the years about the health of local churches. In *To Love and to Cherish from This Day Forward: . . . A Portrait of a Healthy Church* Randy shares his journey. Focusing on the biblical metaphor of the church as the bride of Christ, Randy applies his typical creativity to helping us grow in our appreciation for the church. He helps us evaluate the health of our own local church in light of some specific questions. Do we understand our scriptural identity? Are we embracing our identity by being missional and following Christ's example? Are we yielding to Christ's authority as Lord of the church? Are we developing community? Are we delighting in the Lord through worship?

Randy Millwood has provided a uniquely helpful "portrait of a local church on the road to health." I commend this resource to you so that you can help your church advance to a state of health that will allow Jesus Christ to get glory through your congregation.

C. Ferris Jordan
Professor Emeritus
New Orleans Baptist Theological Seminary

To Love and To Cherish From This Day Forward
...A Portrait of a Healthy Church

Introduction		1
Intro 2.0	(the Metaphor)	9
Section One	IDENTITY EMBRACED	21
Chapter 1	HIS MISSION, *ours* (Being disciples of Jesus who Make disciples of Jesus)	27
Chapter 2	HIS MISSION, *ours* (...while we are out and about)	33
Chapter 3	HIS MISSION, *ours* (...when we are with the family)	45
Chapter 4	HIS MISSION, *ours* (...what's a family to do?)	57
Section Two	IDENTITY EXPRESSED	73
CHAPTER 5	HIS EXAMPLE, *ours* (Servants who Affect others)	77
CHAPTER 6	HIS EXAMPLE, *ours* (A Practical Look)	89
CHAPTER 7	HIS COMMUNITY, *ours* (It's an Image Issue)	107

CHAPTER 8	HIS COMMUNITY, *ours* (Deep Fellowship and Real Friendship)	121
CHAPTER 9	HIS AUTHORITY, *ours* (Making decisions by Discerning and Submitting)	137
CHAPTER 10	HIS AUTHORITY, *ours* (Discerning and Submitting in the 21st Century Church)	151
CHAPTER 11	*our* DELIGHT, HIM (Worshipping and Adoring Him)	169
CHAPTER 12	*our* DELIGHT, HIM (Gathered *and* Scattered)	185
CONCLUSIONS		199

INTRODUCTION

I was introduced to Jesus by His Bride...

Born in a country that made allowance for the free expression of religion, in a part of that country that leaned Christian in their primary religious roots, into a family of churched people, it was all but expected that I, too, would choose Christianity as my own faith expression. That's how it all started....

The stories of Jesus were referenced as life lessons (positively) or warnings (negatively) all of my childhood. I saw my parents read the Bible together and heard them pray at times. My folks paid for me and my brother to take piano lessons, taught by a Christian man, so hymns and gospel songs were held right alongside classics and pop music as all important to learn.

We were taken to Sunday School, Vacation Bible School (VBS for you insiders), gospel concerts, subjected to Christian radio/TV, driven by nativity scenes at Christmas, listened to Easter cantatas. Even the public school system included a prayer – to God, in Jesus' Name – over the intercom system every morning.

Pastors preached, teachers teached, deacons deaced – all around us, all the time.

When I was ten years old I found myself thinking, okay, this seems to work for my folks, but it is still their faith system. Should it also be mine?

To Love and to Cherish from This Day Forward

That year, ten years of inculcation collided with a good old fashioned 'you're going to go to hell' message at VBS. I went straight to my VBS teacher and said, "not me – no how... what do I need to do here?" She led me through what I would later hear called 'the sinners prayer' and we celebrated my 10 year old decision.

It took me two years (that was 20% of my lifetime back then) to decide if I wanted to be publically identified with Jesus and His Church and, if so, which Church. The traditional way of celebrating a decision for Christ – and of adopting one into membership for the churches I was considering – was through what they called believers baptism – by immersion. I did not swim and was afraid of water. I even took showers to keep from sitting down in the tub. Both the decision and the submission were big deals for me.

At twelve years of age I bobbed out into a lake in north Georgia (if I'd been 3 inches taller I'd been perfectly square, so bobbed is the operative word) where I submitted myself to what was for me a bold and terrifying experience and waded out of the water as a member of the Church of my parents.

I continued to be introduced to stories of Jesus, principles for living from the Bible, and examples via the flesh and blood people who made up the Church, universal and local. Over the next three years I grew into adolescence, which included new ways of thinking – what Piaget called abstract thinking. That personal development happened concurrently with the *Jesus Movement* – what some authors consider the last great awakening in America.

Along that way I was introduced to a new term – one I felt drawn to: Lordship. The description seems almost comical to me nowadays... back then we used the phrase *making Jesus*

LORD. If He is LORD, I cannot make Him LORD. Maybe we should have said "surrendering to Him as LORD" but Americans – even during the conflicted historical era around the Vietnam War – were uncomfortable with that word surrender. So we said "make." And at fifteen, that is exactly what I did. As best I knew at that stage of life, I fully surrendered to Jesus.

One more stop: sixteen. A great year, really – driver's license, free from being a freshman, and (for me) I started dating the gal who became my best friend; my best contemporary human example of love and grace; and my partner for life.

In Church we held the PHP (paid holy people) model of ministry... the big guy up front had a bit more oomph than the rest of us... you wanted him praying if you were sick or in trouble... you went to him for counsel in all matters of life and love... and, yes, him was always a him in our tradition. The idea that all believers were priests, serving the LORD, got all caught up in a sort of church culture caste system with an office, a credentialing process, professional organizations to belong to, conventions of colleagues to attend, and the list goes on.

A collision of multiple worlds: a sixteen year old + a serious relationship + a school system asking: What will you do when you graduate – meets church. With fear, respect and a heart that longed to submit to those in spiritual authority over me, I surrendered to vocational ministry... a career and life trajectory.

Finally, my whole life was given over to Jesus and it only took 6 years. I tell people that I *became* a follower of Jesus from my 10th to 16th years, through the influence of His Bride – the Church, and by a series of incredibly important decisions.

I have since that time continued to follow Him... sometimes up-close-and-personal, and sometimes at a distance – never because He has turned from me or on me, but because of my own ups-and-downs. However, I here confess...

...*the deeper I fell for Jesus, the more disenchanted I became with His Bride*

I hate to confess that – I really do. I like for people to like me (maybe not a 100% people pleaser, but darn close). And I'm afraid you (1) won't like me; (2) will judge me; and (3) will have no interest in what I have to say. But, from the outset, I figure I should at least be honest – authentic.

I remember the day that I realized that my love for the Bride was starting to falter... it was winter 1991. It was a Thursday – early in the morning. Let me tell you the story.

I was by that time a graduate of a Christian college and had attended two Christian seminaries, accruing three different degrees from all of that. After over fifteen years of serving a number of local churches in a variety of Church settings, I found myself in the job that all of my seminary buddies dreamed of. It was a large and influential Church in a state capital in the South.

Like other churches I had served, the congregation believed in a single definition of success: GROW. They held staff ministers to this standard of success. And I *was* meeting *their* standard – the numerical growth of an increasingly complex institution we called the local Church.

It is sadly funny looking back on those years... no Church I ever served asked about the health of the Church I was leaving. Almost everyone wanted an accurate accounting of the numerical growth of that Church. Truth be told, most had already researched the growth factor before contacting me.

I had been a believer for twenty-two years and in Church all my life. [Remember: It was the Church that had introduced me to Jesus.] But I had come to see Church as an organized institution, driven by programs, managed by managers, reaching communities by marketing, and identified by location, signs, and buildings. I would not have said it in those words, but if you had followed me around for a couple of weeks, you would have concluded from my activity that these were my perspectives – my values.

> **The number of meetings to make decisions to direct programs to evaluate attendance to determine success in order to have more meetings was exhausting.**

While Church… the Bride… existed to facilitate the living of the Christ life, that assignment was swallowed up by the complex demands of doing Church work. How your Church, as an institution, performed against other similar churches – or against her own past – was *the* standard of success. For me, Church had become hard, laborious. The number of meetings to make decisions to direct programs to evaluate attendance to determine success in order to have more meetings was exhausting.

After a particularly long Wednesday filled with staff meetings, logistic concerns, worker enlistment driven by lines on an organizational chart, statistical analysis, planning meetings, dinner meetings, prayer meeting and hall meetings, I went home. Exhausted. Barely able to tuck my kids in bed and kiss Adele before falling asleep.

Thursday was my day off (which most often meant I only worked 8 hours instead of the usual 10 or 12 or more). Adele got the guys up and off to school. I stayed buried under the covers. Finally I drug myself out of the fog, looked at her and said, "If this is what God gave His Son to die for, I am not sure I want to follow Him any longer."

As I write those words, I remember the event vividly. It could well have turned my life in a tragic direction. I could have become anti church or worse, anti God, cold, cruel and cynical. I think if you knew my friends they would tell you that is not what happened. What did happen however, was a real season of soul searching – research – contemplation – experimentation. And by season I don't mean a few days, weeks or months. In many ways I am still in the midst of it.

This book represents a stop on that journey. What I am thinking today. It is certainly not a final word, nor a comprehensive word. It is just a word.

I hope in these pages to paint a picture for you; a portrait – one of a Bride which is not an institution, but who is a sort of person. A person made up of many people (parts)... people around the world and across the ages, to be sure. But because I am so finite a creature, I will limit my thoughts to the local expression of that eternal and wonderful person... the Bride of Messiah... the Church.

Why write? I am troubled about the Bride – the Church – about her health.

Don't get me wrong, I am confident in the LORD's ability to keep His Bride – to present her as He intends – to ready her for the wedding celebration. But I live in the here and now and what I see here and now, so often, makes my soul restless.

I once heard that Billy Graham was accused of setting the Church back fifty years. His response to the charge was an apology, indicating it had never been his intention to do so… 2000 years, yes; fifty years, no. So some friends and I spent some pretty focused time on an adventure with Matthew, Mark, Luke and John, and their accounts of *The Life and Times of Jesus* as well as the experiences of His earliest followers. Our goal was pretty simple: imagine the beauty of the Bride and along that way, identify healthy signs of life in that community of saints; those who believed and followed.

The journey carried us to a paradigm that was new to us… being, not doing… not a slogan, but a way of living. We saw how the earliest followers sought to imitate Jesus. It seemed to us that their meetings were mostly driven by something like: "What did Jesus do? Let's do that!" Simple.

This book is a snapshot of that focused time of study and a lifetime of experience.

So, turns out, it's not really the Bride with whom I've become disenchanted.

After years to think about the personal dilemma that launched this journey, I have come to see that it, in truth, was never the Bride with whom I had become disenchanted – it was the way she was adorning herself in my world and this time – focusing on stuff that didn't seem to really matter. In the pages that follow I want to paint a picture of the Bride of Messiah, locally envisioned. I hope to start a conversation (to continue a conversation, really, that many have started through the ages). I hope to compel all of us to just stop for a moment... to get off the *Church-As-Merry-Go-Round*... take a deep breath... and to make the hard decision to look into the mirror of our Church and compare her to this portrait of a healthy Church. At times we will and should smile. But you may also identify an area or two to focus on this next year. Wouldn't that be great... if next year at this time your local expression of the Bride of Jesus was closer to the image of Jesus? I think that would be His goal. I know it is mine.

Intro 2.0
The Metaphor

HERE COMES THE BRIDE

Before there were *Buff Brides* (a TV show about getting in shape before your wedding), or *Bulging Brides* (a similarly themed show on a competing channel with slightly more... well, bulging brides), or *Bridezillas* (a show whose producers advertise, "...where brides go from sweet to certifiable..."), there was *Here Come the Brides*.

Here Come the Brides was a western TV show from the late 1960's. The show was based on a bit of history around the town of Seattle. Now known for angst filled, Goth attired, rock-n-roll punkers throwing back enormous amounts of caffeine; as well as for Microsoft; big airplanes; great seafood; misty rain; and incredible views, Seattle was the logging center of the post Civil War USA. Guys went from all over the country for the work and the money. But the rainy days and lonely nights led to widespread depression, with men quitting to return back East.

Enter Asa Mercer. Mr. Mercer came up with a solution: recruit marriageable women. He headed back East and persuaded eleven ladies and one father to accompany him back to the Northwest. Once there he secured for them a variety of jobs and waited for nature to take its course. If Mercer were floating this idea today, it would likely be to TV execs about a new reality show.

Recruiting – arranging jobs – waiting ... that was pretty much the strategy. The brides went to the grooms.

The title of the show, *Here Come the Brides* was a play on the popular name of the "Bridal Chorus" from Richard Wagner's German romantic opera, "Lohengrin," to which the bride marched down the aisle to the groom. Brides still come to the grooms but my how times have changed.

An occupational hazard of vocational ministry is the wedding. I have been to or officiated at weddings where the newlyweds rode away in a horse drawn carriage in Disney fairytale fashion, all the way to a ceremony where the bride was escorted down the aisle by her Scottie (not someone from Scotland or James Doohan, but a Scottish Terrier in a doggie tux, although a doggie kilt might have been more fun).

One of the things I've noticed through the years is how *much* more complicated weddings have become and how much more expensive those complications are becoming.

The journey of many of today's brides really does make for great reality TV. One simple Google search and I found 237 zillion websites with checklists for brides. Here is a short list of the kinds of things today's brides (and to some extent grooms) plow through for that one special day:

- select a date
- hold the date card (and the competition for who will design it)
- engagement parties
- choose a theme
- choose colors
- make 'who will pay for what' decisions
- choose attendants
- start the guest list
- find a place (usually 2 places nowadays – 1 for the ceremony; 1 for the reception)

To Love and to Cherish from This Day Forward

- revisit your guest list
- select a florist
- select musicians (a string quartet?, a full band?, a DJ?, a harpist?,... a friend who'll play harmonica?)
- shop for/select a wedding dress
- choose the caterer
- choose the photographer
- purchase wedding insurance (I'm not kidding: some sites indicate the average wedding in the USA costs about $27,000, so you might want to protect yourself against such crises as horrific weather, illness/injury, a no-show preacher, vendors who mess up the date…there are also 'riders' you can purchase to cover interruption due to military service, the gowns/tuxedos get damaged, the gifts, liability for guests,… whew! But, no wedding insurance I found offers any assistance for exhaustion, or cold feet.)
- plan the honeymoon
- shop for/purchase the bridesmaids gowns
- start making 'wedding favors'
- arrange for a tasting with the wedding cake chef
- plan the rehearsal dinner
- make the final wedding cake design decisions
- revisit your guest list (why is that ex-second cousin-in-law still on the list anyway?)
- get in shape… see the opening of this part of the book for some TV recommendations ☺
- make wedding transportation arrangements
- design and order the final invitations (including arranging for a calligrapher)
- select the grooms tux
- secure the wedding rings
- get gifts for all of the wedding party
- give a list of must take photos to your photographer

- o finalize the wedding menu (remember, some guests are allergic.)
- o write your vows (or at least print them off the Internet)
- o attend bridal showers
- o make arrangements for the wedding hair/make-up
- o take care of state requirements concerning securing a license
- o send announcements to the local newspaper
- o revise your guest list ("has anyone died, or gotten sick since we started this?")

I'm tired. I'm going to stop. According to the site where I found this list, you are still 1 month out with plenty left to do (including revisiting the guest list!).

These are all things the bride is supposed to manage while she is still living life... going to work, visiting with friends, eating a meal, sleeping. It is no wonder the phrase *bridezilla* has become part of our vocabulary. All of this and still the bride marches down an aisle to the groom.

BACK IN THE DAY...WAY BACK

Justus was a good and honorable man. He was a potter by trade... I guess technically he was an apprentice potter. Justus' dad had been a potter all of his life. As a little guy, Justus would watch, from a safe distance, of course. The results of the craft were way too fragile to have munchkins running about.

The two disk pottery wheel was a blast to play with when the area was otherwise empty – stretching his legs as far as they would go and using his feet to push with all his might, young Justus could just barely make the top wheel revolve. But, just barely was enough. From there his imagination took over and

Justus could craft anything his mind could dream – fine pieces produced in thin air.

Later, after synagogue school was complete, Justus was invited into the family business. He worked with his father out of their family home, drying, firing and, of course, selling all sorts of wares... bowls, goblets, cups, pitchers; large, small, simple, intricate... it was all there.

A little later Justus' dad began to teach his son how to properly spin the wheel – throw the mud – add the little detail the consumer looked for – in short, how to turn his job into an art form and a living. Justus excelled in his newfound career. The artist in him blossomed and the family pottery shed became the place to replace broken pieces or upgrade from wood to fine pottery (Ye Olde Williams & Sonoma).

Justus was incredibly gifted and focused. His dad was extremely proud. Everything was going great until Selah walked into the pottery shed that day.

Her family members were also craftsmen, making small musical instruments for a living. Her dad loved music – song – dance. So when he looked down into the face of that tiny little girl nearly seventeen years ago all he could think to name her was the sweet sounding musical term, *Selah* –sacred; stop; listen long and longingly.

And that is exactly what Justus did when he laid eyes on her: stopped – suddenly – while the wheel was spinning – while the mud was wet. Oh what a mess! I think no one in the shop that day will ever forget mud slugs flying everywhere and the blush on Justus' face. Selah sure wouldn't.

She began to come by more and more often (seems like her family was replacing lots of slightly damaged pottery) and he worked on making better 2nd, 3rd and 4th impressions -- better than his first. Interestingly enough, he also developed a sudden and previously unknown enthusiasm for music. Both of those new habits fall into the category of "things that make you go hmmm...."

After only a few months of this, Justus confided to his dad that he was pretty sure Selah was the one for him (something everyone in the family and all his friends had known since the great Mud Mess Monday, as it had come to be known). Frankly, Justus' dad was relieved. Maybe, he thought, we can start moving things back to normal around here.

But, before that could happen, protocol had to be observed.

Justus' dad made an appointment for a formal visit with Selah's dad. Though not close by any means, they had known each other through the years. So after a few pleasantries, dad asked dad. That's right. The proposal was from Justus' dad to Selah's dad. He proposed a covenant of marriage be established between Justus and Selah and with that, the negotiations began.

What price would Justus' dad pay to Selah's dad for her hand in marriage? Fortunately their acquaintance and respect for each other led to a short and amicable give and take which was, in the tradition of the elders, sealed with a glass of fine wine and a toast!

With the formal contract completed, Justus was free to ask Selah to be his bride – something he did immediately – clinching his end of the pledge with a gift – a ring – one he designed (ah, the artist) and a friend who does silver work forged – BEAUTIFUL. Selah cried. Justus mixed laughter with tears. Friends and family cheered! All of this was done in front of witnesses to make sure that Selah did not seem to be under duress. She, you see, really did have a right of refusal all along... Justus would have it no other way... he wanted her to want him as much as he wanted her.

From that moment forward everything changed for Justus and Selah... well, everything except the home address. **Betrothal began.** It was a *not quite* relationship. They *were* married by *every* legal definition of the term – short and sweet. They were not pretending when they would introduce each other as "my husband" or "my wife." But, Justus and Selah did not live together. They did not consummate their marriage, at all, really! Actually, this was a season set aside to learn to love each other deeply – to depend on and trust each other fully – to become one in the more intimate sense of the term. To be set apart for one another (literally. sanctified).

Being young people, this was their first marriage, so there was much to do to prepare for what everyone called the "home taking."

For Justus, there was a home to build. His buddies, brothers, and cousins all pitched in to help him out (sort of like an Amish barn raising). Gifts trickled in, in the form of time, supplies, and, of course, much needed money. Justus' dad was patient through those months, allowing him to work reduced hours at the shop but making certain he didn't lose that gift of his.

For Selah, there was preparation as well. **While Justus was preparing for life, Selah was preparing for Justus.** He was now her everything! She did see him, of course, but there was a very special seeing him yet to come. After the wine, the toast, the promise and the ring back at the beginning of the betrothal, there was one more thing: the date. It was the date that Justus would come for Selah. Her heart was fixed toward that moment when all of her dreams would become her reality.

During those passing months, Selah was absolutely true to Justus – no flirting with other subtle suitors. In spite of the fact that she still lived exactly where she had always lived, with the very same people with whom she had always lived, she had an identity adjustment to make. She was not just Selah anymore; she was Mrs. Justus. And it wasn't just a name she doodled in her papyrus journal; it really was who she was.

For her there were gifts as well. Wedding attire had to be secured and a hope chest had to be filled – filled with all the latest and greatest cool stuff one would need to set up house in that new home Justus was building for them – for their future family. I wonder... will the new papa-in-law give them a discount on a set of pottery?!

For Selah, she lived in the moment, readying herself by every decision, every behavior, every emotion, for the future – a future that was as real as real could possibly be. **She had to embrace a whole new identity, and she had to grow in expressing herself in light of that new identity.**

Finally, though long expected, still surprisingly soon, the day came. Okay. Actually, it was the night. Since the new day began with sundown, who wanted to wait any longer? Justus or Selah certainly did not.

Selah was home with her folks... cleaned up, dressed up, dolled-up, accessorized, dreamy-eyed, and incredibly centered. The house was electric with emotion... glancing out the door and down the street over and over. Waiting and watching.

Justus washed and readied himself at the place he had called home for all of his life. Then with his folks, he made his way to her parents' house. Accompanied by ecstatic friends and excited musicians and singers, surrounded by torch carriers lighting the way, off they went... like a Mardi Gras parade of friends and family! As soon as people saw those torches the word spread through the village, "the groom is coming," all the way to Selah's house. Selah and her parents strolled out to meet Justus, to whom her dad gave the gift of his daughter and his blessing... and the parade began again.

The procession through the streets was louder now... and filled with celebration. This mobile party made its way to Justus' house – the new digs – picking up more friends of the couple along the way. There was music. There was dancing in the streets. And there was a feast... I'm talking kill the fatted calf feast, with all the trimmings.

After the feast, Selah and Justus were escorted to the bridal chamber by parents and close friends... a quiet place. With tears and joy the parents gave their children, one final time, to each other. Alone, they went into the room and were physically intimate for the first time.

All the friends and family kept working on the buffet, and waited.

After a while, Justus did what thousands before him had done... he stuck his head out of the tent (with a big smile on his face) and announced with glee, "our marriage is consummated!" Another loud roar from the crowd – more music – more dancing – more jokes – more wine – more food. In fact, their wedding feast lasted over an entire week.

Wow!

DID YOU NOTICE?

I suspect you did, but just in case, in the story I just told, Justus represented the Christ and Selah represented the Church – His Bride. If you missed that, I'll wait right here while you run back through it again with that image in mind.

Did you see the differences from the weddings of today? There are so many, but here are a few:

Difference #1: The story started with the groom's father. The proposal of marriage was a contract – a formal covenant – that started with the father of the groom, in which he paid whatever price was required to secure the bride for his son. Arrangements were immediately made for the time, place and size of the wedding, again by dad.

Difference #2: With this informal, intimate ceremony of sorts, the groom and bride entered into a period of betrothal... a time of acquisition... a time of setting apart (sanctifying). The bride and groom were as committed to each other as any married couple – an arrangement that could only be broken by divorce. There were only a few differences from what was to what would be: they didn't live at the same address and while developing great intimacy, there was a greater intimacy to come. The groom departed with a promise to build his new bride a home and return for her one day.

Difference #3: While the groom was preparing a home, the bride was preparing herself for the groom's formal return and the wedding feast. During this time she remained absolutely true; adjusted her thinking about her identity; arranged for her wedding day apparel; built her hope chest... the stuff she would need to set up home in the new house her hubby was preparing. And she waited – watched – lived with incredible expectation.

Difference #4: Once the bride was ready, the groom came for her. She did not march down an aisle; he marched through the streets.

Difference #5: The procession was public, loud; very joyful... there were friends, family, and lots of food.

Difference #6: the celebration went on a long time....

So, what does any of this have to do with this little book?

It is the stuff of difference #2 and difference #3 that is the concern of this book: how exactly might the Bride go about preparing for the Groom's return? How does she get ready?

I am not thinking about one individual believer here. We are, after all, parts of the Body... each one of us. And I am not thinking about the Church Universal... all believers, from all places, and all times.

In these pages I am thinking about the local demonstration/expression of the Bride of Christ... individual believers, united to Christ and each other, on a local mission... a local Church.

How does a local Church spend the time from marriage covenant with the King to His coming? How do we prepare ourselves for Him? What is our new identity? How is that identity expressed to others?

I have become concerned that for many of us we have gone the way of the typical modern bridal stuff, busying ourselves with similar sorts of issues ... we have focused on what might be considered as externals... gowns, caterers, florists, locations. Or in our case, Church buildings, programs, policies, procedures, and so on.

But, are there other issues... more important issues... that we should be giving our attention to? (Obviously, I wouldn't have raised the question if I didn't believe there are...)

So, with this analogy in mind... the betrothal season...

- the Christ, who is our Groom, coming for His Bride
- the Bride truly married to Him, here and now
- the time of setting apart for each other in play
- His coming for her just around the eternal corner

I want to explore some simple ways that the Bride (a local Church) can prepare herself. I do not suggest that these ideas are ground-breaking, new, unique or comprehensive. Instead, as I've said, I hope to continue a conversation that prayerfully will result in new, formidable and transferable ways of being, for Church after Church.

Along the way we will visit Justus and Selah, using them as an anchor for our analogy.

Are you ready to get ready?

Here follows a portrait of a healthy Church...a local expression of the Bride of Christ... a Church who chooses *To Love and to Cherish from This Day Forward*.

SECTION ONE
IDENTITY EMBRACED

During the year or so of betrothal, Selah faced the incredible challenge of adopting a brand new identity. In her world, her identity was inseparably linked to the man in her life. For all of her life that man had been her dad... Selah didn't regret this fact – she loved and honored her dad.

Don't feel bad for Selah in this regard. She was not only her daddy's baby girl, but she was also seen as someone of inherent worth – someone who bore the image of God – certainly not a second-class citizen. This characteristic is set out in the very beginning of The Story. Although she did not have all the socio-political advantages of the men in her world, she still grew up hearing the stories of her faith, including those of the women who played dominant and significant roles among her people... women like Esther, Hannah, Abigail and Deborah.

One of the first descriptors of her gender in sacred text was that of a help-meet; a companion. And, since companionship is always two-way, she had always seen herself as one part of a greater whole.

Genealogies – a family lineage – were incredibly important to the family. And folks had figured out a long, long time ago that adding generations to that lineage required a female. Selah grew up seeing her mom nurture and care for her and the family and then helping her do so. Given that warm environment, it was only natural that she also wanted one day to be a mom. In fact, the role of mother was extremely valued in her world.

A critical part; a foundational part; of the time of betrothal was a change in her sense of identity – quite literally, a new sense of personhood. No longer was she Selah, the daughter of her father. Now she was Selah, the companion of Justus. This new self was one she embraced; body, soul, and spirit. It was an identity that impacted who she saw herself as (internally) *and* how she presented herself (externally) to others.

And so it goes…

As we – the people of God called Church – merge our lives into union with Christ, we too take on a whole new identity. It is much more than a future thing… it is here, and now… Oh, there's a future aspect… there will be a marriage supper. But make no mistake about it; we are the Bride of Christ right now.

Like Selah however, we come into this new identity out of a former one, a much more familiar one. And like Selah, that former identity is pretty strong. Whether it was healthy (you were raised by devoted followers of Christ who loved you thoroughly) or a bit more challenging (you came to Christ out of a less than wholesome life experience), your former self is very real and must be laid aside over time.

These years of betrothal represent a fantastic opportunity for the Church to embrace her new identity; both internally and as we present ourselves and our Bridegroom to others around us.

Famous Last Words

Perhaps because of an interest in history, or maybe because of simple curiosity, I enjoy an occasional stroll through a good cemetery. (As I re-read that sentence I am struck by how creepy it sounds, but I did spend a number of years in New Orleans, Louisiana where such an activity is actually a tourist attraction. People come from all over and pay for cemetery tours.) It is amazing what you can learn about people from looking at tombstones. For example, the sheer size of the tomb and the opulence of the tombstone will give you a hint as to: (1) their financial resources, or (2) the number of true friends they had or (3) the number of frightened enemies they had accumulated.

Tombstones also make for interesting, sometimes entertaining reading. A pet cemetery in California has a tombstone that reads, "There must be dogs in heaven, 'cause I can't imagine heaven without my dog." A gravestone in England is reported to be that of an atheist whose buddies had engraved, "All dressed up and no place to go." The famous comedian, George Burns outlived his equally popular wife, Gracie Allen, by several decades. When he died they say the couples' tombstone was completed with the phrase, "Together Again." However, my all time favorite headstone is reported to be in a rural part of East Tennessee where an unassuming stone of a long-suffering husband is said to have carved on it, "I told you I was sick!"

Tombstones represent a kind of last words. That is, an enduring message that the dearly departed (or family or friends) wanted communicated throughout generations... something to communicate the real identity of this now-so-empty space. Sometimes those words will literally be the last words of the person. When death comes at the end of an extended illness, people will often carefully consider and plan their last words. The words are generally meant to inspire those who remain. Last words are important to people – to those who hear them and to those who say them.

I would love to have been a fly on the wall during each of Jesus' post resurrection appearances. It would have been interesting to see the faces of followers who suddenly found themselves face to face with Him after witnessing His crucifixion a few days before. I would love to have felt the exodus of oxygen from the room as gasps crashed in black holes of mid-air; to have seen tears well up in the corners of the sun dried faces of true believers.

For about forty days Jesus walked and talked with those who had walked and talked with Him. He repeatedly told people that it was not necessary to be afraid. He led in Bible discussions along the way to Emmaus. He extended greetings and lavished peace. He gave people opportunity to dialog about their own faithlessness and offered forgiveness. He spoke about many different things to a great variety of people.

In spite of the variety of settings and discussions that Jesus was involved in, there was one common theme through all of His post resurrection conversations. Each of the Gospel writers was captivated by it. I don't know if it was the words He chose, the vastness of the vision He cast, or the passion with which He spoke. But I do know that inspired by God's Spirit, every Gospel writer was compelled to record some version of it. They were a kind of last words, important to both the speaker and the hearer.

Mark, noting Peter's account of Jesus' life, described an intimate mealtime where Jesus said, "Go everywhere in the world, and tell the Good News to everyone" (Mk. 16:15 NCV).

Near the end of Dr. Luke's researched report came the story of two followers from Emmaus walking home from time with the eleven disciples. Jesus joined the journey and the homecoming dinner. After His departure, they rushed to tell the eleven what had happened. He again, showed up, confirming their story. There He authorized them and us to serve as His ambassadors, carrying His message to all peoples. "There is forgiveness of sins for all who repent [turn]" (Lk. 24:47 NLT).

Luke's second volume opened with yet another meal (man did they love to eat) with the eleven disciples immediately prior to Jesus' ascension. Trying to help them understand the spiritual nature of His Kingdom, Jesus reminded them to trust His Father with the things that He alone controlled, but not forget matters for which they had responsibility. Specifically he said, "...when the Holy Spirit comes to you, you will receive power. You will be my witnesses – in Jerusalem, in all of Judea, in Samaria, and in every part of the world" (Acts 1:8 NCV).

John described an even more intimate gathering behind locked doors, where Jesus stunned and overjoyed them with an unexpected visit, greeting them with, "Peace." Then He challenged them to live life with a new sense of mission. He said, "Peace be with you. As the Father has sent me, so I am sending you" (Jn. 20:21 NLT).

Without question, the most often cited setting of these last words is that of Matthew. Early on Resurrection Sunday, Jesus talked with some women at the tomb, now with a vacancy sign flashing. He sent them to rally His disciples to a familiar hill in Galilee.

When the disciples managed to get where Jesus was, they saw Him. And when they saw Him they found worship to be the irresistible and natural response (though some of them were still struggling with fits of doubt). Jesus said to them and through them to His Church, "I have been given complete authority in heaven and on earth. Therefore, go and make disciples of all the nations, baptizing them in the name of the Father and the Son and the Holy Spirit. Teach these new disciples to obey all the commands that I have given you. And be sure of this: I am with you always, even to the end of the age" (Matt. 28:18-20 NLT).

Four writers. Five accounts. Perhaps He knew that He would have to repeat the message often for His first disciples to get it. Maybe He knew His future disciples would have a kind of curious fixation on those last words. But maybe, just maybe, He was deliberate in the choice to repeat those phrases over and over again. Maybe He had a last point that had to be emphasized in order to complete His mission.

Whatever the motive, it seems certain to me that Jesus was saying to His disciples and through them to us, that ultimately His Church has but **one identity**: disciples of Jesus. And flowing from that identity, one task: disciple making.

This is a simple, obvious measure of the health of the Bride of Christ – the Church → they (the people of God) embrace that they are all about one thing: being disciples of Jesus who are making disciples of Jesus... a new, real, here-and-now identity that validates itself as we live among those who live around us.

In the pages that follow, let's wrestle with the task of embracing this identity as a Church, as a Bride. I challenge you to join in the practice of throwing off any and all other identities you may hold as a Church – of casting aside any and all other tasks that you give space, time, finances and energy toward.

As Selah was privileged to swap selves – to become a new person – to change how she would invest the rest of her life – so too are we.

Chapter 1
HIS MISSION, *ours*
(Being disciples of Jesus who Make disciples of Jesus)

For Selah this journey from an identity based on the home of her father to one based on the new household of Justus would be guided by critical questions (all good quests are, after all, guided by good questions). Selah must ask herself questions of being before questions of doing... what is it to be Justus' wife – eventually the mother of his children – a companion who helps him meet his mission?

The same is true for the Bride of Christ. If our identity is no longer found in our parents, our hometown, the teams we root for, our jobs, our hobbies, our friends, and so forth, we must ask, "What is a disciple of Jesus?" It is a question of identity: just who are we?

WHAT IS A DISCIPLE?

The word *disciple* was not too uncommon in Jesus' day. There were many disciples of various teachers and schools of philosophy. While the word is not as common today, the concept is everywhere. For example, there are disciples of economic gurus, disciples of certain computer programs, disciples of various sports teams, and disciples of famous people. Today's disciples may be called apprentices, students or fans, but they are everywhere.

Holy Spirit, throughout the Bible, used the word disciple in a variety of ways. In John 1 we are told of the disciples of John the Baptist. In Mark 2 the disciples of John the Baptist and the disciples of the Pharisees are mentioned. In John 9 we read of the disciples of Moses. So, one of the common uses of the word disciple was to refer to anyone who followed a certain teacher or a school of philosophy.

Another biblical use of the word disciple was as a general nickname for *The Twelve*. While larger numbers of Jesus' followers were called disciples in the general sense (for example, see Jn. 6:60 and following), there were times when the word was used only of *The Twelve*.

> **Luke 9:58**

Jesus more often than not used the word disciple in yet another way. He used the term to describe those who were consciously considering the cost of submitting their lives to His rule and becoming a part of the Kingdom of Heaven. He once reflected on the loneliness that sometimes accompanied the decision to follow Him – that sense of separating from what had been so familiar. He likened following Him to being a builder who weighed carefully the expenses of a project or a king who considered thoroughly the costs of war. Having made such an intentional decision, the people called disciples were variously characterized as not looking back; loving Jesus more than family, friends, or self; actually giving up everything for His cause.

> **Luke 14:26f**

Jesus called for an uncommon devotion on the part of those who would choose to become His disciples… those who would embrace this new identity. He reluctantly released those who refused His benchmark, rather than watering down His standards. He carefully modeled and painstakingly repeated that this kind of disciple making was His one mission and must become theirs as well. Did the first Church understand this mission? The evidence of early Church history would lead one to conclude a resounding *yes!*

The first covenanted believers (the Church) so bought into the idea of making disciples as Jesus intended, they were so determined, so effective at making such disciples, that the world around them took notice – not of their attendance, or their buildings, or the pithy sayings on their signs, but of their lives.

In the book of Acts, Luke tells the story of the beginnings of the Church in Antioch of Syria. The incredibly Good News about God's Kingdom and Jesus, His Messiah, had been announced to both Jews and Gentiles in that town. The Jerusalem Church was a little anxious about the Gentile Issue, so they sent Barnabas to investigate. This man, described as a good man, full of the Holy Spirit and strong in the faith, was filled with joy and encouraged by what he saw there.

Acts 11

Barnabas immediately called on his old friend Saul to join him in Antioch for a season of assisting those new disciples of Jesus. They stayed there for a full year with those followers. Over that time a wonderful and remarkable thing transpired. The people in Antioch came to faith and began to grow in that faith. In fact, they grew so effectively that they increasingly looked like Jesus, acted like Jesus, talked like Jesus, and reacted like Jesus.

The pre-Christian people around them began to say, "I'll tell you what. I've seen disciples of this teacher or that teacher… of this school of thought or that philosophy… but these disciples of Jesus are uncommon for certain. They don't just study their faith; they are not just intellectually curious about their Teacher; they act as if they are the very Master they keep talking about. They are like 'little Christ's' themselves… *Christians*." From that very moment on, the disciples of Jesus were more often than not called Christians: disciples who were so much like Him that they earned the right to be confused with their Teacher. As John the Baptizer might have said, they were decreasing and He was increasing.

That is the essence of the disciple making identity for the Church today. To so embrace the values of Jesus and so incorporate His characteristics that people who know us would conclude that we too look like, act like, talk like, and react like Jesus in increasing measure. We are to be that kind of disciple; to make that kind of disciple.

The Church → any Church → your Church – should become increasingly effective in the work of disciple making.

- It does not matter whether you describe your Church as traditional, innovative, program based, Sunday School based, cell based, purpose-driven, organic, elder led or committee led.

- It doesn't make a difference if you are a Baptist Church, a Lutheran Church, an Episcopal congregation or a Pentecostal fellowship.

- It doesn't matter if you own a $21 million Worship Center or you meet in homes around your town.

- It doesn't make any difference if your collective, corporate calendar includes one gathering a week or you have developed a 24/7/365 schedule.

At the end of the day, at the end of the week, **here is the only thing that matters** - - are you growing to be disciples of Jesus making disciples so effectively that they look like, talk like, act like, and react like Jesus, more and more? That is what it is to wholly embrace our wonderful new identity. That is how Jesus spelled success. That is what it is to embrace the role of Bride – the Church.

If this is not *who* you are as a Church – if it not what you do as a Church, who exactly are you? What exactly are you doing? And why are you doing it?

Selah was embracing her new identity throughout her betrothal season, rearranging life, learning a new way of family, responding to her world based on who she was becoming rather than who she used to be.

This is the journey of Christ followers in these years between faith acceptance of Jesus and face to face with Him. Phrases like "take off the old self," "now you are children," "lead a life worthy of your calling," "throw off your former way of living," and so forth, pepper the pages of New Testament letters.

We are called to live differently among each other and among those who have not yet been able to see this incredible Good News up close. The later describes what the Church has classically called evangelism (chapter 2) and the former what the Church has called discipleship (chapter 3). As you read the pages that follow, continually evaluate your own self and your Church in these matters. Have you truly embraced this new identity that is yours – are you being the Bride of Christ?

Chapter 2
HIS MISSION, *ours*
(...while we are *out and about*)

As Selah moved about through her normal day, a lot about her life didn't change. She still saw friends and family on special occasions and in daily interaction. She still prepared and cleaned up after meals. She still shopped many of the same markets. She may have moved slowly from her former role at the musical instrument shop into the new world of her husband's pottery shed, but even there she probably suggested pottery pieces that would be valuable to instrumentalists, bringing in a few new customers.

While logistics may not have changed much, what did change was significant. This new identity soured Selah to present herself differently in the various settings of life. It is really hard to describe. She may have signed her new name to the ancient equivalent of contracts and checks. But it was much more than that. The conversations she listened to deeply were different, what she listened for was different. The emotions she felt were real, what made her heart race was different, what saddened her was new. Her curiosities were changed.

Responding to her world, based on who she was becoming, living differently among those around whom she lived...

It all boils down to identity – how we now see our world and consequently how our world now sees us. I call it disciple making when we're out and about.

DISCIPLE MAKING OUT AND ABOUT

Jesus' prayer in John 17 compels the people of God in any local community to always remember that they live in two worlds. This mystery has application to every simple stroke of the portrait of a truly healthy Church. Each Church does and must function in two worlds simultaneously. We live under the reign of our present and very real King, with our spiritual family through the community of the Church. And, *at the same time*, we live in this flesh and blood world we walk around in day by day... two current and real dimensions we always occupy.

While living in New Orleans we learned that an umbrella was as valuable as shoes and pants... you didn't leave home without one. Every day, for at least 8 or 9 months a year, we could look forward to the hour of shower. My friend, John, was looking at an umbrella resting open and drying in a corner one day, and saw a visual of this spiritual journey we all share.

Imagine that the handle of the umbrella represents conversion... that really big decision, often culminating from a journey of small decisions, to believe what God has said about you, about His love, about His Son... to put the weight of your faith, such that it is at that moment, fully in Him.

All of the ways that a community of faith or its parts engage and relate to people to the left of that handle, the pre-conversion side, represents what might be called disciple making out and about or how we demonstrate our new identity to people not yet connected to our Father, but to whom we have some connection. (If you are a longtime Church person, the word you might think of here is evangelism, but don't run too far ahead with any baggage you bring to that word.)

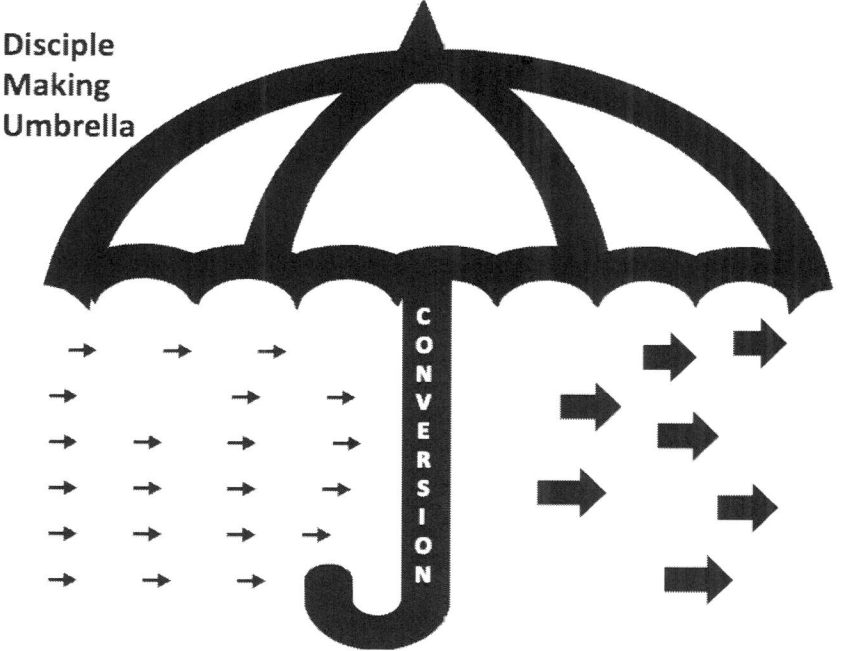

An elementary English teacher once told me, "Ain't ain't a word and you ain't supposed to use it!" American English, like American culture, has become a unique blend of various words from all over the world. Often our culture will adopt a word from another language, create a match of our alphabet for theirs, then pronounce and use the word popularly without translation. For example, many of my friends from the Southwest will part company by saying, "Adios!" and some of my Euro-urbanite friends like to say good-bye with a hearty "Ciao!"

This practice is known as transliteration and the American Church has joined in the fun on many occasions. One such word is that word evangelism. Evangelism is a Greek word that has simply been spelled out in English. Actually the word for evangelism is really more of a blending of several words found in the New Testament. The noun form of the word is usually translated Gospel or Good News. The verb form of the word is sometimes translated: to preach or proclaim or announce or to tell.

So the word evangelism represents a very comprehensive set of ideas rather than one single action. My general definition of evangelism would be everything and anything that the Church (the people of God) does in order to show, describe, announce, or explain the Good News of Jesus. It is to help others in their process of hearing and reacting to God's gift - God's Kingdom now available in Jesus Christ. In that respect, evangelism should or could be to Christian people as natural as breathing... as you and I inhale God's wonderful grace and mercy it is the most natural thing in the world to exhale this Good News. Healthy communities of faith find those who spiritually breathe best (those who excel at disciple making while out and about) and arrange for them to help those of us who have a little spiritual asthma when it comes to breathing out.

BENCHMARKS AND EXERCISES ALONG THE WAY

Pre-Conversion

Pre-conversion people can be found along a great continuum at different points on the journey toward conversion. While some may be at the doorstep of making a decision to submit themselves to the peace filled reign of Christ in their lives, an increasing number are much farther away. Some are near a new birth event, others are struggling with the implications of such a change in their lives, still others are trying on Christianity through relationships or practices, and some have barely even conceived of the idea that they too could become followers of the Christ.

A large and growing number have started their spiritual journey at other places and are not yet engaged in a relationship with a Christian person who is being supernaturally transformed. If you want to see this visually, turn back to the disciple making umbrella and imagine the arrows to the left of the handle as all of these people... some close to conversion (the handle), others far away. Now put some faces or names from your life on those arrows ... people you know who are at these various places along spiritual quest.

American culture may have been more Gospel friendly in previous years. Things such as public nativity scenes, Easter holidays, public prayers, and posted Bible passages certainly provided pre-Christians with more data about our faith. Culturally Christian European immigrants and an agriculturally based dependence on a supernatural power made it rare to find someone who did not know someone who believed in the God of the Bible, so relationships built the bridge into Christianity.

History however has marched on and circumstances have changed. Industrialization, urbanization, multiculturalism, post-modernity and a host of other factors have contributed to the secularization of American culture. None of those changes caught God by surprise. They may have broken His heart, but they didn't surprise Him.

The Church should not spin her wheels in the sand, lamenting the loss of advantages once held exclusively and only because of the larger culture (ah, the good old days). Instead, a Church must adjust pre-Christian disciple making in order to continue to communicate this Good News of God's Kingdom available in

Christ. Some even propose that this post Christian culture of ours could actually put the Church at an advantage. The opportunity to capitalize on the newness of this wonderful faith adventure and the incredible God who orchestrates it all is ours for perhaps the very first time in American history. Wow!

Post Conversion

While pre-Christians are at different points along the way to a relationship with Christ, those who follow Christ are at different points along the journey toward Christ likeness. A few, sometimes loud believers, have gotten themselves stuck by assuming one method of evangelism is THE method of evangelism. When that method fails to produce the harvest they envision, they turn inward or blame the culture's deterioration or criticize churches that attempt new methods or sadly, just blow off someone who is loved by God – someone who is a prisoner of God's enemy.

Claims such as these have usually revolved around methodological approaches such as lifestyle evangelism, service evangelism, relational evangelism, verbal (explaining) evangelism and confrontational evangelism. As you might expect, there have been (and continues to be) passionate spokespersons for each of these views. Multiple articles, tons of books, a growing number of training tracks, and teaching Church conferences have argued for their approach as THE approach. The general presentation almost always makes its way back to assert that their approach to evangelism is the approach that Jesus used. The arguments might go something like this:

Confront them!

Jesus was a confrontational guy. In John 8 He encountered a woman accused of adultery and confronted her with her own sinful ways demanding that she, "Go on your way. From now on, don't sin…" (Jn. 8:11MSG). When face to face with a wealthy, young, religious ruler (someone obviously impressive to the Gospel writers), Jesus demanded that He sell all of his stuff and follow Him. He confronted synagogue rulers, religious leaders, friends, followers, seekers and saints. Confrontational? Indeed.

Explain it well and they'll get it!

Jesus used verbal explanations of the incredible Good News that He came to bring. John 3 contains the compelling story of a courageous, religious seeker with sincere questions who, for reasons not fully explained, preferred to protect his anonymity for a season. While Jesus could have refused him or ridiculed him, He chose to meet with Nicodemus, engage him in conversation, illustrate the Kingdom of heaven and explain theological concepts like condemnation and God's love. It seems in fact that Jesus was constantly explaining the Kingdom of Heaven to those ready to be engaged – telling stories, clarifying misinformation, risking reputation to bring revelation. He was it appears, a polished verbal explainer/evangelist.

Get to know them!

Oh no (some would say), Jesus was actually a relational evangelist. He sought to destroy the social and class barriers of His day. When a Samaritan woman came alone to the community well, Jesus disregarded a class barrier that said Jewish men don't speak to Samaritan women (Jn. 4). When the local tax man went out of his way to see Jesus, Jesus refused to listen to the disparaging eyes of the crowd breathing down His neck as He initiated a conversation with this tax collector (Lk. 19:1-10). In fact, Jesus seemed to delight in the accusation that, unlike other so called messiahs, He was a friend to sinners.

> **Matthew 9:11f and Matthew 11:19**

One of the two primary charges that His opponents repeatedly brought against Him was that He kept on eating and drinking with sinners – hanging out with Matthew and the boys – relating to normal folks.

May I serve you?

Servant evangelism advocates see Jesus the social worker (and they make a convincing argument). Early in Jesus' public ministry, He announced a strategy for evangelism from Isaiah 61:1-2. The text was all about announcing Good News by serving the poor, the imprisoned, the handicapped, and the socially disadvantaged. That prophecy, He said, was fulfilled *in* Him that very day. For the next few years Jesus supported His verbal claim by feeding hungry crowds, touching untouchable lepers, and freeing people captured by various addictions. In fact John wrote that should anyone attempt to pen down all that Jesus said and did, the books of the world could not hold the script. He was a busy Messiah – constantly involved in serving people and by so doing, drawing them toward an encounter with Himself that could potentially change their lives.

Live it = Give it!

Lifestyle evangelists claim that others have made evangelism too complicated. They point to an evangelism approach that rested in Jesus' model of a redeemed lifestyle. Walking around, living life as a redeemed person, compelled others to inquire. Mark frequently noted how crowds, captivated by Jesus' life, would throng after Him. Matthew mentioned a woman who suffered for a dozen years with hemorrhaging. She knew of Jesus' life and reputation and thought to herself, "If I can just touch his robe, I will be healed" (Matt. 9:20 NLT). Luke told of a Roman officer who understood authority and recognized that Jesus had it (Lk. 7:1f). Nicodemus began his conversations with Jesus by admitting, "...*we all know that God has sent you* to teach us. Your miraculous signs are evidence that God is with you" (Jn. 3:2 NLT, italics mine).

People were attracted by the way He lived. They enjoyed spending time with Him. They were challenged to want to live differently by His example.

And so the argument has ensued: Was Jesus a confrontational, verbal, relational, service or lifestyle evangelist? The answer is: Yes!

If Jesus, the One who demonstrated all of what it is to walk in the Spirit... gifts, fruit, whatever; saw value in variety, does it not stand to reason that His Bride should see similar value? Should we not approach our disciple of Jesus identity in our engagement with pre-Christians as more of an art (with many expressions) and less of a science (with some elusive right approach)? Can we just listen to Holy Spirit as He guides us to be appropriately engaged with friends, family, work associates, neighbors, strangers, and so on? Can we trust like that?

Being disciples of Jesus who are making disciples of Jesus should not be tied to focusing on, learning, mastering, and implementing some method or program that involves six Green Beret Christians out of a congregation of 200, who have drilled their method for so long that they could repeat it if you woke them up at 2 AM. It is much more natural than any such thing; much more comprehensive; and requires so much more of you and me – a level of compassion and concern; a willingness to defer our mission for His; a depth of self denial we have perhaps never dreamed.

Our efforts at being disciples who make disciples when we are out and about dare not be separated into a stand-alone ministry of the Church reserved for a few individuals. When the contemporary Church segregates evangelism into an independent program of her institutional format, we become content with addition, fixated on those churches that add best, and we lose the New Testament concept of reproduction, which results in real multiplication.

Imagine a congregation of 200 followers of Jesus, who are communicating the Good News appropriately forty hours a week while at work, additional hours while involved in community recreational leagues, more time as they set the standard for being a friendly neighbor, and even more as they sit and enjoy spiritual conversations with friends and family. Imagine a Church that actually equips people to be like that – to live like that rather than training them to participate in and manage a program that is headquartered in a building most pre-conversion people will never see the inside of.

The example we have in Jesus is making disciples while out and about – a sort of prenatal process, culminating in a birth; something eternal in quality; life that has meaning. Evangelism is the faithful partnering of the Church with Holy Spirit to intentionally move people toward Christ. That process can and does happen in every arena of life. The actual new birth could occur at an office or factory, a home, in the car, during vacation, anywhere and anytime.

But to focus on the birth itself as all that disciple making is about, could be missing the point of His commission. Jesus could have chosen to say, "Go make decisions" but He did not. His commission was inclusive of decisions, but bigger – much bigger.

By focusing on the process rather than the results, a Church can become much healthier in her identity as a disciple of Jesus, the Groom. Think of a runner who runs for the fun of it rather than one who runs because some doctor told them they ought to for their health. The latter only notices the cramps, muscle aches, and sweat because they are only thinking about the result. When they achieve whatever their goal is, they stop. The former embraces a new way of living – a new sense of identity. They don't run, they are a runner – and that makes all the difference in the world.

The Church (the Bride of Christ) can become more intentional about partnering with Holy Spirit and investing in people from as far from God as you can imagine, all the way to as much like Christ as one can be in this world. We can serve those who need to be served, build relationships with the lonely, explain Good News to the curious, challenge those who are stuck, and love them all. We can move with them through the door of conversion and stay alongside them as they begin to mature in Christ. This is not the whimsical daydream of some baby boomer idealist. It is the mission and lifestyle of our Christ and His earliest followers.

But in order to live out a new identity while we are out and about in our world, we will have to lean into a new identity as we relate to one another… in the spiritual family of our local Church.

Chapter 3
HIS MISSION, *ours*
(...when we are with the family)

Selah's new expressions of her becoming identity – how *she* saw her world and consequently how they saw her – found root and encouragement from this wonderful new family she and Justus were creating. It was in that context – at home – that she learned to see herself differently. It was a safe place for her to try on this new self – to falter without failing. If her family relationships were decidedly dysfunctional, the way she demonstrated this new identity when she was out and about would be equally dysfunctional. So it was important to be the bride inside the family as well as outside.

The same is true for those of us who follow the Christ. We are adopted into what is an ancient, but new to us, family – a timeless spiritual family – and a very up close family (our local Church). It is in our new family that we too find the roots and encouragement that allow us to express this new identity among those still outside the family. It should also be a setting that allows us to try on who we are becoming in Christ – a safe place to falter without fear of failure.

If we miss who we are as a spiritual family, if we accept some second-class, culturally shaped version of it, we will not find the courage or the roots that we long for and need. Our identity will be a little schizophrenic, as we live/behave according to one set of standards when we're with the Church and a different set when we're elsewhere. This is self defeating to the Church and dangerous to the spiritual health of those who are watching us.

But if our Church honestly embraces our identity and the role of helping each other live it out, our behavior will more naturally demonstrate to those around us who we are becoming, and Who is shaping us. They will not just see the change (external) – they will be inspired by the transformation (holistic) and want to know why... how... what... WHO!

THE NEWS

Jesus was always very selective in His use of words – His Spirit was equally selective in His inspiration of which of those words would be written down in the Bible. In those powerful and persistent final words of Jesus to His followers He said, "Go and **make disciples** of all nations...." As I said before, He did not say make decisions or make converts. Instead, He carefully chose words that communicated a strategy which He had used in His own ministry and which He would use to multiply His life through others, spreading this Good News to all people everywhere.

News has degenerated to an always negative word in our culture. Good news is not real news to most media outlets. If it is reported at all, it is reported as the 'just before we say goodnight, fluff story' of the news. Journalists would tell us that serious correspondents bend over backwards not to be saddled with those stories.

Our family has lived in the shadow of cities across the USA – places like Detroit, Kansas City, New Orleans, Washington, Baltimore, and Atlanta. Over the years local news has caused us to become sadly familiar with how cheaply some people view life.

Violence escalates all around us. This is probably true everywhere in the country, but living in those cities as parents of kids then of teens, we were most aware of those local news reports. What seemed like responsible adults (according to their neighbors) would, under the influence of alcohol, take the keys of their car and drive down an interstate highway, becoming a parent's worst nightmare. Young people desperate for drugs would snuff out the life of an innocent tourist in the hopes of finding enough money to get their next fix.

The reports are everyday occurrences in most cities. However, upon occasion, we hear about a truly bizarre practice – something that shocks us, even in the midst of a bombardment of sad news.

While our kids were teenagers we were stunned to hear stories of young girls who would get pregnant and somehow manage to hide it from everyone around them. Their boyfriends did not know. Their parents did not know. The school officials did not know. Their employers did not know. They actually hid a pregnancy for 9 months.

I am not certain what the motivation was. Perhaps they were so young and so scared that they somehow convinced themselves that they really were not pregnant. Maybe they were certain that they could not go through an abortion. Maybe they were entertaining the idea of running away and raising the child. Whatever went on in their brains, the rest of the story was almost always horrible beyond description.

Very often these young girls would give birth to the child, alone in an alley or school bathroom. Then they would carefully and tightly wrap the child, placing him or her in a garbage can or dumpster... maybe they were hoping a rescuer would come to the baby, maybe they were not thinking at all. Once in a great while the story ended with a hero or heroine hearing the whimpers of the struggling child and liberating them. Too often, the story ended tragically. *It is just so hard to believe that a young parent would simply abandon a defenseless infant to the elements.*

When a Church deserts a new born Christ follower, they are guilty of following the same practice as the young teens just described. **They are spiritually abandoning an infant.** They are turning incredibly Good News into a sad postscript.

This was never Jesus' intention. His plan was the holistic, whole life transformation of a person, as demonstrated by His own model. Disciple making while we are out and about is what we have called evangelism. Disciple making when we are with our new, spiritual family might be called spiritual formation or discipleship. It is the inseparable continuation of the disciple making quest! It is the flip side of the same coin… and you cannot spend half a coin.

DISCIPLE MAKING WITHIN THE CHURCH FAMILY

On one side of the door of conversion is the life of curiosity. On the other side is the life of the convinced (not without doubt, but faith convinced). The goal is for every believer to mature until s/he reaches the full image of Jesus Christ. Paul said it (Col. 1:28, Eph. 4:13). Peter assumed it (1 Pet. 3:13-15). James called for it (Jam. 1:4). John was concerned about it (1 Jn. 3:1f).

The evidence of the watching world around the early Church was that they did it (Acts 2:47; 11:26). However, while every believer is to walk this path, no believer is to walk it alone.

Many churches today have lost sight of the comprehensiveness of this one task – being God's partner in announcing Good News, drawing men and women toward Christ and adoption into His family, then connecting them to their new spiritual family in which they are increasingly shaped into His remarkable and increasingly unmistakable image. This is the task of disciple making. This is the one and only thing that the Church is commissioned by Jesus to do.

> **Disciple making is the one and only thing that the Church is commissioned by Jesus to do.**

Do you remember the umbrella image from the previous chapter?

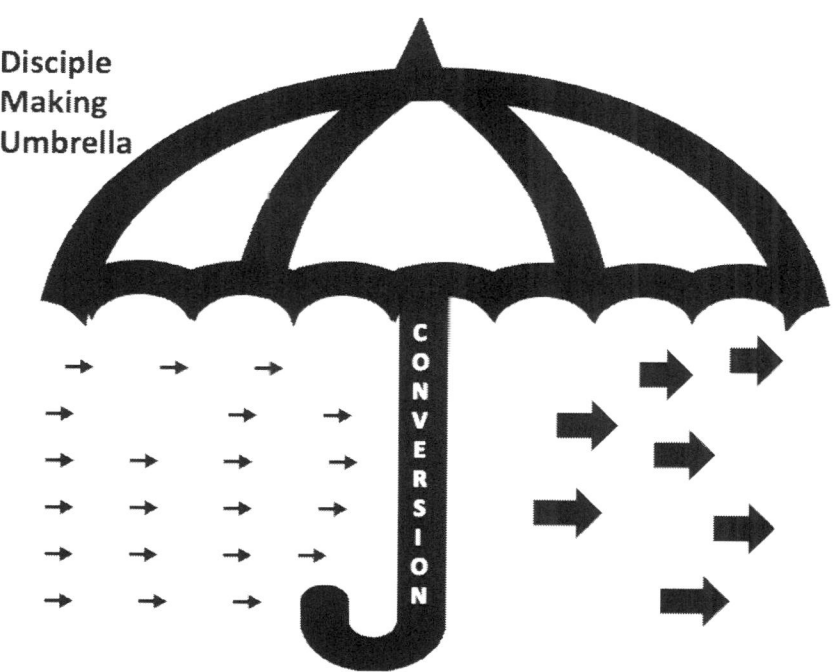

Disciple Making Umbrella

As you recall, the handle of the umbrella represents conversion. All the ways that a community of faith or its parts engage and relate to people to the left of that handle, the pre-conversion side, represents what the Church classically calls evangelism.

The arrows to the right side of the handle represent the post conversion process... all of the ways a faith community (a local Church) engages each other... the ways we spur one another on (as the writer of Hebrews said)... the ways we assist in forming this new and real identity increasingly toward the remarkable image of Jesus.

As a boy, one of my favorite games was "Simon Says." The game is pretty tame for younger kids, but it can get brutal to the serious "Simon Says" contestant. While the challenge may increase, the basic rules do not change. Simply stated, IT gives a command. If *Simon Says* precedes the command, then you must obey IT immediately because IT has assumed the authority of Simon. You are not to filter the intelligibility of the command, you simply respond. But, if IT gives a command that is not preceded by *Simon Says*, then you must ignore the command.

Sometimes you will have a tricky IT who attempts to confuse you by modeling an action that they have not, under the authority of Simon, commanded you to do. Even in those deceitful circumstances – don't obey or you will lose.

The game has only two basic players. There is IT who may assume the authoritative role of Simon at any time; then there are the contestants. As soon as a contestant is called *"out"* they become a part of the peanut gallery, a kind of accountability section, keeping an eye on everyone else. Their passion becomes catching someone else failing.

Christian maturity is certainly not as elementary as a game of "Simon Says," but it is in some ways as simple as a lifestyle of "Jesus Says." Just like in the game, what others say does not matter ... but what Jesus says is not to be questioned. You simply must obey. In the game the leader will often call out a command that sounds unusual to you. If you question the instructions, you are likely to lose the game. In a similar way, it is not nearly as important that you fully understand all that Jesus says at this moment, but it is imperative that you recognize the sound of His Voice and spend your life **obeying** all

> *We obey toward understanding, not insisting we understand before we will obey.*

that He says. It is how all of us learn as kids – we obey toward understanding, not insisting we understand before we will obey (that is considered rebellion). It is an act of trust – a willing submission. It is learning by experience, or applied knowledge. It requires relationship and results in intimacy. And the family is the place for both.

There are a couple of noteworthy differences in the "Jesus Says Lifestyle" and the game of "Simon Says." In the game, IT has the right to attempt to trick you by providing an oral command and a visual demonstration while not assuming the role of Simon. That kind of trickery or deceit will never be found in the Master *and* should not be found in His Bride – the Church. Attempting to hold and impose on others some theoretical accountability standard for a way of living that we fail to model ourselves is unacceptable!

Secondly, in the game the accountability factor is the negative result of competition. All of the people around you carefully watch your every move and spring on you if your actions are not obedient to Simon. Through the Church, Jesus has provided a wonderfully positive form of accountability. People walk with each other, watch over one another, and hold each other accountable to live as Kingdom citizens in this foreign land. This is the essence of what it is to grow up in Christ: to obey Him, demonstrating we love Him, thus becoming more like Him. The Church is the family in which this journey advances.

MORE ON THE WORD DISCIPLE

The word translated disciple in Matthew 28:19 is the Greek word *mathetes*. This word might be literally translated as learner. In the twenty-first century, climbing out of modernity, we visualize learners through the lens of contemporary, formal education. We imagine desks (or chairs and table), marker boards, computer screens, lectures, presentations, content, exams, and experts. We presume the intellectual right to contemplate what is said and select what, if any, to integrate. We think of discipling as mastering a subject. And we totally miss the point.

Mathetes describes learning accompanied by endeavor. The idea of a skilled craftsman guiding the nervous hands of an apprentice comes to mind. The learning of content was the fringe benefit of changed behavior. And the behavioral change was motivated by a new set of values and passions, literally a new sense of identity. We seem to have the right pieces in mind these days, but we get them out of order.

I grew up in an era when television included a number of variety shows. Those entertaining shows usually had at least one comedian each week. Some of those comedians were impersonators. That is, as a part of their act, they would take on the persona of a public figure. Sometimes that only meant their voice. Most of the time it meant changing their hair, contorting their face, exaggerating some tick, and even dressing for the part. It was apparent that those entertainers had spent hours reviewing tapes of their target and standing in front of mirrors until they virtually became the other person. This, ultimately, is the idea of the disciple of Jesus. A person would be so consumed with the Master that they would find themselves doing as He would do. Not in the shallow way an entertainer impersonates someone, but in the rich and meaningful way that a child imitates their parents. Not that they know everything that the parents know But they long to be everything that the parent is.

When my oldest son Josh was 3, we lived in West Virginia. Those hills were cold to this son of the South, so I started wearing corduroy pants to the office instead of dress slacks. [For the record, corduroy was very stylish in West Virginia at that time!] It wasn't long before Josh needed a pair as well... he called them his "work'n pants." He didn't have a firm grip on what exactly I did. But because we were family, he wanted to imitate me.

Children tend to impersonate their parents for two basic reasons. One has to do with a deep respect for the model of their parents. This is imitation by choice, appearing in very young children (like when a little girl dons her mom's heels) then reappearing and developing in healthy situations as we mature.

The other has to do with shared DNA. Bill Cosby hilariously tells the story of standing in front of the mirror as a young adult, washing his face, peering up through sleepy eyes then screaming when he saw what looked like his own father staring back at him. This is imitation by design.

People who are believers in Jesus Christ share His DNA through the presence of His Spirit. As they grow up toward Him, they naturally (DNA) and consciously (respect and love) choose to imitate Him more and more. To mature as a disciple you see, is not to master a subject, it is to choose to be subjected to the Master.

Disciple making is a lifelong self denial, follow ship of the Master. It is the intentional, disciplined journey toward Christ likeness. It is the choice to become clay in the Potter's hands, allowing Him to mold and craft us increasingly into the image of His Son.

Maturity is not an option for a believer to entertain; it is a command to arrange life around. Eugene Peterson wrote about the saw-toothed history of God's people in the Bible (*A Long Obedience in the Same Direction* 86f), and to be sure, our journey continues to be filled with ups and downs. But it is always moving forward toward holiness... otherly-ness. It is coming to seek first our God and God's Kingdom. It is growing to surrender personal goals to God's goals. It is acting, reacting, walking and talking more and more like Jesus.

> **To mature as a disciple is not to master a subject it is to choose to be subjected to the Master.**

This kind of maturing process does not happen in a vacuum anymore than the pre-conversion stage of disciple making takes place without a great host of witnesses. Instead it requires the nurture, encouragement, education, warning, and accountability of a spiritual family - the Bride of Christ, the Church.

Did you know Jesus did not tell the Church to teach disciples everything that He taught? He didn't! But He did command them to teach disciples **to obey** everything that He taught.

Now that's a whole other thing. That's huge. The sheer scope of such a demand must drive us to our knees, seeking His power, and to His example, seeking some compass to guide us.

As impossible as it would have been for Selah to create a new identity apart from the new home that she and Justus were forming in her world, it will be impossible for us to embrace our new identity without the roots and encouragement that we should find in our Church family.

As great the risk that Justus and Selah took – the risk of creating something dysfunctional – the risk that any new family takes – even greater is the same challenge before the Church. We dare not buy into discipling strategies that are weak and incomplete.

However, the wrong strategy is not the problem for most churches. In my experience the real issue is that churches have absolutely no strategy for the post-conversion making of disciples. Those who do have a strategy seem to lean toward one of three very limited and one-sided approaches. Want to know what they are? Read on.

Chapter 4
HIS MISSION, *ours*
(...what's a family to do?)

The family is the place to experiment with, nurture, correct, instruct and embrace this new identity being formed all through the betrothal period. That was true for Selah and Justus. It was true for their friends and family. And it is true for the Church as well.

Selah and Justus were running a huge risk; starting a family. What if they got it wrong? What if they performed so poorly in their relationship to each other that any sons/daughters they brought into the world were destined for some dysfunctional reality TV show on down the road?

It was more than a risk; it was a grand adventure as well. The coin flips both ways you know. What if they got it right, or at least right enough? Imagine the joy of bonding with your soul mate – of celebrating the births of children – of watching them grow and mature. It was a risky adventure to be sure, but well worth it.

This is the journey of the Bride – the Church – as well. To form as a spiritual family requires that we take risks. But to do nothing... to dig a hole and hide the treasure God has given to us... that is totally unacceptable. So here we stand – looking into the future, charged with embracing our new identity in Christ, with walking through conversion all the way toward His remarkably unmistakable image. But how do we do it? What does that look like from inside the family?

In my experience, most churches seem to own and defend one of three incomplete models to achieving this monumentally important assignment ... post conversion disciple making.

THREE STRIKES, YOU'RE...?

<u>The Woodshed</u>

The woodshed was an outbuilding on any pioneer American farm, including my grandparents' farm. At first it was a place to store wood for the fireplace and stove. With so much wood in one place, it came to be used as a workshop for small, wood related building projects. In time this isolated, quiet, somber looking, stern room filled with ample rods of correction became the ultimate timeout corner... a place of punishment.

One model of disciple making implemented by lots of churches is the woodshed model. This view of spiritual growth holds that there are certain behavioral standards for a believer in Jesus. Where I grew up the old timers used to quip, 'Christians do not drink, cuss, dance or chew; or go out with girls who do!'

It is certainly in keeping with Jesus' example to expect high standards. But this approach usually does not consider it important to understand why you do or do not do what you do... why you are sent to the woodshed.

In fact, the most extreme versions of this model might openly degrade any efforts to understand. For example, such an approach might require a new convert to immediately be baptized because it is an important act of obedience (and it is). Yet little or no attention might be given to helping the convert see and embrace the rich symbolism of this obedient worship of the LORD. The only message sent is, "If you love Jesus, you will comply."

In the woodshed, disciple making strategies almost all revolve around lists of do's and don'ts. Some may lean toward the positive (like the baptism example) but many find their way into negative territory. Guilt becomes a valued and frequently used motivational tactic in such a setting. If you fail to meet the standard, well, there's always the woodshed... shame, embarrassment, ignored, shunned, or even dis-fellowshipped.

The Classroom

The 180-degree pendulum swing reaction to the woodshed might be called the classroom approach. This enlightenment era – age of reason – modern design of disciple making – values learning as an academic discipline, almost to an extreme. Advocates of this approach are convinced that the more you know, the more mature you are. Everything is a study for them.

They often look down on behaviorists as uninformed, a little ignorant, unenlightened, or spiritually immature (wanting to place a virtual dunce cap on them as they sit in the corner of the woodshed). The plethora of Bible study resources on the market today both targets the advocates of this model and delights them. The completion of one study is always followed with the inevitable and ultimately exhausting question, "What's next?" "Who wrote the next book?"

In this approach, the spiritual journey is sort of like the pursuit of academic degrees. As with the woodshed model, a measure of truth makes this model appealing. Without question Jesus was well studied/practiced in the customs of His faith.

Additionally, Holy Spirit, through Paul, encourages believers to avoid ignorance and to study their new faith – their new identity.

The Garage

A third approach to disciple making in many American churches is what I call the garage model. It is built on an osmosis approach to spiritual growth. This view sees spiritual maturity as tenure in the Kingdom, or more specifically, time at a certain local Church.

In the most extreme versions of this approach it does not matter how much or how little someone might know (classroom model). Nor does it matter how you act when the Church is scattered or gathered (woodshed model). All that matters is how long you have been around.

The model looks like this in a Church: someone (anyone) holds a role of influence in the Church family... (a role that should require spiritual discernment) but they hold the post primarily or only because they have earned the right to do so by putting in their time. The old adage is, "Being around a Church no more makes you a disciple of Jesus than hanging out in a garage makes you a car." However, this model is built on the notion that maybe it does.

Once more there is some truth here. Much of what it is to be a follower of the Christ is better caught than taught. Therefore you might assume that hanging around the Kingdom, over time, should result in some spiritual growth.

As you can imagine by now, I am rather strongly convinced that while each of these views in their milder perspectives holds a measure of truth, all three are incomplete. This conviction is based among other things on the deficient way each views a believer.

- The woodshed sees the believer as a machine, performing functions and deserving punishment.

- The classroom holds that the believer is a student, making the grade - or not.

- The garage envisions the believer as a club member who puts in their time and earns the right.

Jesus, however, saw followers as children of God, His friends... members of His Father's family... His Bride. We have been given this new identity and with it new responsibilities toward one another. Our pieced together models – whip them into shape; teach them to master the subject: just hang around long enough – they all seem right for their own reason, but not really whole. So how do we embrace this identity and our new family?

SEEMS LIKE TIME FOR AN ILLUSTRATION

New Orleans is sometimes called America's most unique city. It is certainly the most unique town we ever called home. In New Orleans there is no north or south. Directions are given toward the river or toward the lake. The west bank of the city is at times south and even east of the central business district. And in New Orleans you do not *shop* for groceries, you make groceries!

Make'n Groceries is more than shopping – it is a comprehensive and community way of living. It includes deciding what you need before you go, enjoying the company of friends while you are at the market, and cooking some of the finest food this side of heaven with the prize of your hunt.

People start *make'n groceries* early in life in New Orleans. Kids participate with parents, grandparents, extended family andneighbors. The idea is that when the kids grow up, they will be able to pass this little piece of culture along to the next generation... and they'll be able to eat well all their lives.

Adele and I have two wonderful sons, Joshua and Caleb. They are both adults now and our best contribution to the next generation. Apart from salvation, God's greatest gift to us has been to know them and walk through life with them. One of our constant goals as parents has been for them to grow to the point that they would not need us to survive; to reach the point where they could make groceries all on their own.

While *make'n groceries* sounds like a little thing, it is not in the greater scheme of life. It includes the ability to develop a balanced and healthy menu, smartly shop for and buy groceries, store the bounty correctly, select from a variety of inspiring recipes, prepare the food properly, serve the meal attractively, sit down and use the right utensils and etiquette while eating the meal, embrace the intimate community of a shared meal, clean up appropriately, put the dishes through the dishwasher and return them to the shelves. Then once you've finished, get ready for the next meal.

If we had used a woodshed approach to reach this goal, Josh's and Caleb's childhood would have looked something like this: from the very first spoon of baby cereal they would have been punished for failing to get the food in their mouths or rewarded for success. They would have been trained to mechanically lift their spoons to begin the journey then return them to the tray without incident. As they grew older, they would have been led to master increasingly difficult skills with more complex tools (forks, knives, even sporks!). Punishment would have been designed for failing to repeat the desired behavior. Reward would have been designed for appropriately repeating the desired behavior.

While that system might have been helpful early on, ultimately they would have moved from infant/toddler to become children. By that point, every other word out of their mouths would have been "why," but the only answers our model embraced would have been, "Because I said so!" or, "Just trust me."

Again, this might have quieted them for a while, but childhood gives way to adolescence. The natural, God given desire to become independent during those years could only have been interpreted as rebellion by the woodshed puritan. Our goal as parents would have been to break them much like a rancher would break a horse – before the horse whisperer. If we succeeded, then the young adult would step out into the world able to do what we set out for them to do with one notable exception. They would only have been equipped to go to the same stores, buy the same food, prepare the same menu, and clean up in the same environment. Their behavior would have been the same as that of a machine. Their ability to transfer that behavior to other settings…to grow… would have been greatly limited.

If we were inclined toward the classroom, then we would have done most everything for them until they reached a pre-determined age. Then one day we would have sat them down in rows in the living room and pulled out a set of charts and graphs for use on the family overhead projector. First, we would have reviewed a mock menu. The menu would have been used to talk to them about the different kinds of foods in the food pyramid and the importance of balance.

After the lecture we might have engaged them in some exercises where they put together menus, followed by Grocery List 101. Some hand-eye coordination would have come by clipping coupons. A grocery store floor plan via PowerPoint would have guided a simulated learning activity. Being good teachers, we would have divided all of the lessons into units, appropriately tested them along the way, ceaselessly looked for new literature resources, moved on to the next lesson when they passed, and provided certificates to note their mastery of the subjects.

If we used a garage approach, then Adele and I would have done everything for them. Their only job would have been to hang around. We would have prepared every meal from a warm bottle to a piping hot, homemade pizza. We would have designed every menu without their input. We would never have bothered them with shopping trips and nutritional information. Instead, we would have simply said, "Trust us." We would have ignored their behavior at the table and excused them from every meal to their own fancy while we cleaned and returned everything to its place.

Upon their graduation or wedding, we would have reluctantly passed the baton to the next generation, giving them a full set of our dishes, our pots and pans, and our utensils (after all, they were good enough for us – why should they need those new fangled kinds). Sending them on their way absolutely convinced that they had been around the food chain for about twenty years so surely they were ready to take up the mantle themselves.

Sound crazy? It really is not that unlike the halfway strategies of most churches when it comes to post conversion development.

The woodshed almost always results in people who are, in a way, independent. Yet they are totally dependent on the environment remaining unchanged – unlikely in food preparation; inconceivable in disciple making. Both the local Church and the environments in which we dwell are changing, ad infinitum. A Church that makes disciples like that will sit around and lament the loss of the good old days, defensively huddle in a shell and criticize the very world into which they have been sent.

The classroom builds people who have the intellectual information but not necessarily any operable skills in Kingdom living. In a Church, people like that come back over and over to the same well of information, or worse yet, set a goal of being that information man/woman for others – pointing people to me instead of to Him. Their constant cry is, "Feed ME!"

The garage approach results in people who are living a fantasy – not prepared to make the kinds of decisions that result in a good, healthy diet. And the garage Church? They are living a fantasy as well. Simply being around it for while—paying your dues – does not automatically equip you to discern God's vision for a congregation, decide how to properly steward the Kingdom resources God has made available, or make disciples of others.

A DEVELOPMENTAL PERSPECTIVE

More like the comprehensive and community living example of *make'n groceries*, the spiritual family of the Church must find ways... structures... systems... to merge instructing (classroom), correcting (woodshed) and unconditionally loving (garage) into a holistically safe place to embrace our new identity in Christ.

The word that comes to mind when I think of this is development – a pretty organic kind of thing. As you read through these next few paragraphs I want you to let your mind toggle back and forth between what will look normal to you in life and dream about how it might look in Church.

All believers come into God's Kingdom the same way: through birth. Infants *and* babies are cool. But babies do not make a productive contribution to enterprise. The truth is, they do almost nothing for themselves, to start with. If they are healthy, then the important internal functions operate naturally... their hearts beat, they breathe, and they digest... oh do they digest!

However, who would carry a new baby into their home saying, "Now Sally, here is the fridge. If you need some milk, we keep it right here in the door. Of course the milk is cold, so let me show you the microwave. It's really pretty simple to operate; just set a time and push the start button." Just the opposite is true. We do not expect infants to care for themselves. In fact, most new parents delight in the total dependency that this precious little child has on them. However, should infancy persist into adulthood, there is a problem.

Nursery aged children are a bundle of energy. They grow so fast in those first years and that growth is easily visible to those around them. If you are a relatively new grandparent you know what I'm writing about. Just go a few months between visits and that little one seems like a whole different person. During those short years s/he learns to sit, crawl, stand, toddle, and walk. They are potty trained and learn to feed themselves. Communication moves from screams to sentences. They do not learn any of this by themselves or without multiple failures. Yet with great persistence (and varying degrees of patience), parents endure every fall, every additional diaper, and every green pea on the floor, in the hair or on the wall!

Grade school aged children seem to develop in spurts: slowly, then suddenly. They vacillate between total dependence and growing independence. The mobility discovered during the nursery years finds total expression in bike rides, swimming and skateboards. The safety of always being home is sacrificed for the adventure of school and sleepovers.

With adolescence comes a whole new world of maturation and mountains to climb. The disequilibria of the nursery years seem to return as physical, emotional, intellectual and social growth occur at different times. The pressure to be yourself wages a daily battle with the pressure to conform to others. The door hinge between childhood (with great dependence) and adulthood (with demanded independence) swings back and forth at an alarming, roller coaster rate.

Young adulthood brings the apex of physical strength and the low rung of the vocational ladder. The ability to reproduce yourself and the desire for real intimacy takes center stage as marriage and establishing a family becomes an important part of who you are. If you have had a healthy relationship, your parents move from guide to coaches/mentors for your journey. Additional helps are discovered and mature and intimate relationships are established with new friends.

Middle adulthood and older years bring the advantage of wisdom accumulated by experience to bear on the lives of others around you. Growing comfortable with who you are makes for a more relaxed person. A concern to invest in others finds expression in almost everything you do. You have moved from being an infant, totally dependent on others, to being the wise guide for those who would raise up a new generation to be interdependent with others.

Did you see it? It is normal, healthy, developmental growth. The family is the setting. Along the way people are instructed and instruct; they are corrected and correct; they are loved and love.

Post conversion disciple making is simply (not easily, but simply) a super*natural* developmental process. Some believers in every Church community are infants, others are nursery children or grade school children, others adolescents, young adults, or maturing adults in Christ. This view is certainly not new. John the Apostle, writing under the inspiration of Holy Spirit in his first letter, referred to those who are children, those who are young, and those who are mature (1 Jn. 2:12-14). These stages are not something to be achieved and rest in - they are processes – short tours along a grand journey.

There is a really important paradigm here that I do not want you to miss: **a developmental view means spiritual formation into the image of Jesus is normal and natural.** It takes time. It is something God is doing (He is conforming us). And it takes a family. **No one matures in a healthy fashion alone or in a crowd.** There are behaviors imitated along the way. There are ah-hah moments through the experiences of life in Christ. There are lessons learned over time in the journey. But ultimately, to make disciples, the Church will need to see believers as people, children of God, friends of Jesus, on a journey from total dependence on others to interdependence with others *and* total dependence on Him. Such a journey does not happen in a woodshed, a classroom or a garage. It will only happen as a family, in relationship, on mission.

Anyone who has ever raised more than one child knows by experience that there is no one-size-fits-all way to do this. Two kids, with the same parents, the same basic DNA and the same nurturing environment are still so incredibly... unique. As long as a Church – any Church – your Church exhausts man hours and creative energies trying to find that one-size-fits-all model, you are likely going to just run around in circles and kick up a lot of dust.

So, what do we do? Well... love each other, unconditionally; instruct via example and mutual submission; expect folks to grow; have the kinds of relationships that give permission to challenge any lack of growth; and measure by fruit... results... not by how well you used the method

> *If you wonder about the fruit, go ask neighbors and folks at work. Either they see it or they don't.*

(whatever that might mean). By the way, if you wonder about the fruit, go ask neighbors and folks at work. Either they see it or they don't. It really is that simple.

Our churches are different. The gifts of our people are different. The needs in our various communities are different. The learning styles of our people are different. The relational personalities they default to are different. Different. Different. Different.

We have a common destination: the increasingly unmistakable image of Jesus. But we are all as churches and as members of a Church starting at different places. **One-size-fits-all will never**

exist. I am pretty sure that would be God's standard too. You see if there was a system, we would all depend more on it than on our great God... it would be easier... require less from us.

Ultimately all of these differences will require unique spiritual formation maps for each Church. A strategy for spiritual formation will never be truly final any more than a strategy for raising a child is final. It will always be changing as the congregation and the neighborhood around us changes. We must keep our eyes fixed on the goal... Jesus. And we must create an environment that nurtures honest assessment of where we are, toward that goal. Finally, we should hold no model so tightly that we would not immediately release it at the first sign of failure to result in the fruit our Father seeks... the remarkably, increasing image of Jesus.

A FEW MORE RANDOM THOUGHTS ABOUT DISCIPLESHIP

While every Church likely has an innate sense that they should be making disciples through this wonderful period of betrothal; most have not stumbled on a way to do so. There is a massive difference between moving people through a system and submitting to God's Spirit as partners – a partnership where He guides and conforms people toward the image of Jesus Christ.

In the former, the focus is on a system that can become complex, cloudy, and the center of our attention and affection. The people become merely the fuel to keep the system up and running.

In the latter, the emphasis is on the people and their plain and simple devotion to Jesus. There are plenty of systems, but their value is only to the degree that people are actually growing toward Christ... as witnessed by people around them.

Churches that seem to be healthiest do more than talk about the importance of people growing up in Christ. They have a strategy for helping each other mature into the image of Jesus. This strategy is uniquely conceived, well designed, carefully articulated, passionately implemented and ceaselessly evaluated by the fruit of a person's life rather than by the process itself.

I think this is an important reminder to us that, while salvation IS free, it IS NOT cheap! This concept is essential to the development of a strategy of maturing people into the image of Jesus Christ.

- It ought to be extremely easy for people to come and observe what Christians do when we gather for worship or study or when we scatter and fellowship or serve.

- It ought to be extremely natural for believers to build meaningful relationships with pre-Christian people, witness to them through word and deed, scatter seed and bring in a harvest.

- BUT, it ought to be extremely clear to those who are drawn by the Holy Spirit to Christ that HE DESERVES EVERYTHING.

Now, what of the relationship of this spiritual family to the world around us? Simple: Christ-like behavior will always ensure that disciples are investing in those who do not yet know Him. That is where He spent His time. That is the mission to which He was called. That is the mission on which He has sent His Church. **If people claim to be maturing in their faith, but are not concerned for and involved in the lives of those not yet reached, you can be sure of only one thing: They ARE NOT growing up to be like Jesus!**

CONCLUSIONS

The first beautiful stroke on the canvas of our portrait of a healthy local Church – an expression of the Bride of Christ – is recognizing and embracing our new identity, which is found in being a disciple of Jesus who makes disciples of Jesus.

This task demands that every Church ask and answer two significant questions: "What *is* a disciple?" and "How do you make one?" Ultimately a disciple of Jesus is someone who so values Him that they are cooperating with His Spirit – adjusting their very lives to be like Him in every way. Their progress is visible to those around them. To the Corinthian believers Paul described the idea like this: "I don't want anyone to give me credit beyond *what they can see in my life or hear in my message*..." (2 Cor. 12:6 NLT, italics mine).

While I have argued there is no one way to achieve this, I do believe Jesus used strategic means in making His very first disciples. They are more general than how to, but real nonetheless. And because of their organic, generic nature, I think they are transferable to *any* local church. What follows is in many ways my general answer to the question, "How do you make a disciple?" I think you will find here additional touches for the emerging portrait of the Bride of our Christ.

SECTION TWO
IDENTITY EXPRESSED

Selah's big challenge for the time of betrothal was adopting a brand new identity. This meant seeing herself (from the inside, out) as a new person... a new creature.... and it meant others around her would begin to respond to her – relate to her – as this new person (from the outside, in). It was a massive identity reconstruction process.

Justus kept his identity, but he had some tasks he was working on during the period of betrothal. There was of course the tiny little detail of a home to be built. It is likely that he built this on the property of his family, maybe even as an extension of their house. You see, he *went away* as it were, from Selah in order to *prepare the room*. Once it was completed he would *come again and receive her to himself*... the wedding feast would begin. (If those words sound familiar to you, read the first few verses of John 14 about the *Life and Times of Jesus*... it is a beautiful picture.)

This was also a time of proving... a time in which again and again, in a million ways, Justus showed his betrothed bride that she could indeed trust him to provide for her every need. It was a time where her faith in him grew and grew.

The word identity comes from the Latin *identitatum*, which literally means sameness. We tend to think of it today as having to do with what makes one unique among others, but it actually speaks to what makes us *the same*, at all times, regardless of our circumstances.

To Love and to Cherish from This Day Forward

Identity formation for a betrothed couple is the process of developing both a distinct *and* corporate personality... something that is the same, no matter where you are. It has a constancy about it... it is solid and can be trusted.

Betrothal was a time for this rock solid identity to be formed, then to be expressed. It was the merging of souls, absent the cares associated with physical union, resulting in an unshakable foundation on which to build a life together. It was a time of (literally) sanctifying – of setting self aside to be joined to another. It was a time of mystical union (abandoning a passing identity in favor of a new, emerging identity).

It was also a time to accomplish some legal and very practical kinds of things. Most of these were Justus' responsibility – establishing the home, establishing his business, demonstrating his faithfulness, and so forth.

But Selah had a few things to achieve as well. She received and organized gifts; she prepared her wedding attire, readying herself; and she demonstrated her fidelity and loyalty to her new husband.

And so it goes...

As we (the Bride of Christ called Church) merge our lives into union with Christ, we receive His gifts, order life, and demonstrate our fidelity and loyalty to Him. It is a journey that takes time and involves more than a few ups and downs. Fortunate for us, we have a profoundly forgiving Groom who is incredibly patient along this way.

Like Selah we address these responsibilities with devotion, but out of a lifetime of habits that may not altogether match our new identity. The behaviors we exercise, the habits we practice, will be replacing former behaviors and habits. And like any new activity, will take time and practice as well as require a support network.

Selah was surrounded by people who were pulling for her in this quest. We too are surrounded by a great cloud of witnesses. And as a part of this forming Bride of Christ, we are surrounded by real people in the real world of our local community of faith.

The question is not "Are we forming and expressing a new identity?" The question is "How do we do this?" A peek into the example and model of Jesus as He interacted with His little community of faith (the guys we call *The Twelve*) gives us good insight into some of the practical ways we can as a Church express our new identity, readying for the wedding day.

In section two of this book, I will introduce you to four ways we can express that new identity. I don't pretend to suggest this is comprehensive, but it is simple – it is consistent with the model of Jesus and the example of the first local communities of faith that sought to follow that example – and it is doable. So read on. And as you do, lay this template over the Church you belong with. Use it as one tool to help decide what you no longer need to be doing on the way to expressing who you really are.

CHAPTER 5
HIS EXAMPLE, *OURS*
(SERVANTS WHO AFFECT OTHERS)

It was a night to remember. The stars were blinding laser beams piercing through the tiny holes of a three dimensional sky darker than coal. Had the word been invented, everyone in the room would have likely called the evening electric! It was a climactic moment in a week of mountain top experiences. A dramatic and extravagant anointing preceded a royal procession unlike anything the city had seen in generations. It appeared that the people were now set to rally around this once-and-again controversial teacher. The outpouring of love and devotion had stunned even His closest followers. Astonishing signs and bold teaching almost certainly guaranteed that the time had finally come. The politics of Rome would soon be supplanted by the long anticipated Messianic reign. Now, it was time for an evening of celebrating the past and preparing for the future... strategy planning.

The room had been miraculously provided and meticulously prepared. Every morsel was carefully cooked and set in its proper place and order. The evening was ready to go off without a hitch. Then, a hitch showed up. While the bowl, water and towel were carefully laid beside the entryway, someone had neglected to secure a foot washer. This hitch may sound minor to you and me, but to people who actually reclined at a table set low to the ground, dirty feet meant the pleasant aroma of the meal would be suffocated by the smell of hot, dusty, sweaty feet – in this case – twenty six filthy feet!

The question crackled through the room like the rustling of leaves on a windy fall day: "Who will wash feet?"

Will it be Peter? Likely it will not. After all, Peter is large and in charge, bigger than life (at least in his own eyes). Everyone knows he is Jesus' Number One. What would they think if he were to abdicate the throne of leadership in order to wash feet? No, he is not likely to do it.

How about John? Will he wash feet? John is called *the beloved*. It is an endearing nickname to him and to Jesus. But he knows the other disciples sometimes treat him like Joseph of old was treated after receiving that new coat of his. He is, tonight, the one who leans on Jesus' shoulder. He has a special relationship with Jesus. If he moves from the table, someone else may slip into his place. So he is probably not going to wash feet.

How about James? Will he wash feet? James is John's brother. Together they are known by the handle, *Sons of Thunder*. That could be because their dad had a bad temper. Likely it is because when they rubbed elbows, it was like two contrasting air masses colliding high in a storm cloud resulting in a clash called thunder (serious sibling rivalry). As long as John sits there, unmoving, James is not about to wash feet.

Would Matthew wash feet? He has certainly seen it done before. He knows how, at least by observation. He has been affluent enough to own or borrow a foot washer or two in his day. Perhaps that is the very reason he doesn't move. He has seen how foot washers are treated; ignored as they bow at the dirty feet of preoccupied people.

Could it be Thomas who will wash feet? I doubt it. He once rallied the troops claiming that if Jesus was to die, then they should go to Jerusalem and die with Him. But a martyr's death and foot washing are two entirely different matters. In one case, you are a hero; in the other, you are a zero. "No thank you."

How embarrassing. This room was supposed to be completely prepared. *Somebody* dropped the ball and whoever moved first could be admitting that he was the one who missed an assignment. A competitive jockeying for position raises its ugly head once again. The winners are the ones who get their feet washed. The loser is the one who bows to peer pressure and washes feet. The question is never, "Will our feet get washed?" for the Passover meal cannot be dishonored by dirty feet. The question is, "Who will wash feet?"

John wrote how with confident assurance Jesus slipped from His seat and glided over to the corner with an unassuming manner. Once there He removed His coat and tied a servant's apron around His waist. Deafening silence draped the room. He poured the water into the basin, then turned and started toward the disciple nearest Him.

> **By the time Jesus came to Peter, Peter had finally stopped looking at everyone else's feet and started looking at his own.**

We are not told of any conversation between Jesus and eleven of His followers. He simply performed the duty of the servant, silently and resolutely washing feet.

We are however told of one conversation. By the time Jesus came to Peter, Peter had finally stopped looking at everyone else's feet and started looking at his own. Mortified by the condition of his feet (and maybe by the condition of his soul) and confused by the idea that Jesus would hold them, wash them, and dry them, we are told that he protested. Not much of a surprise; Peter often protested.

"What?" he says, "You can't wash my feet. I am not going to let you. Not now. Not ever!" To this challenge Jesus gave a puzzling response. He said, "If I don't wash your feet, you are not one of my people" (Jn. 13:8 NCV). That is, if I can't serve you, you are not a part of me. If I am not your servant, I cannot be your King.

A servant King?

A leader who serves?

I am fairly certain Peter didn't get what Jesus was saying. I am absolutely certain that I still wrestle with conceiving of such a notion. However, to Peter's credit, he did change his mind. In fact he made a swift and total paradigm shift. Here's how I would paraphrase the conversation, "LORD, if that is the case, then just give me a shower! Start with the hair and go all the way to the toes." It seems that Peter was genuinely confessing that he wanted to be a part of Jesus... to be one of His people (whatever that might involve) and if to do so meant permitting Jesus to bathe him, then so be it. Jesus pragmatically responded something like this: "Peter, you don't need a shower. You've already been bathed. The problem right now is your feet stink. I know it. You know it. And the people sitting near you know it" (Jn. 13: 9-10).

The most telling imagery of this whole encounter followed that rather practical observation. **Jesus washed Peter's feet.** The snapshot is one of the most revealing moments ever captured from the life and times of Jesus. Here in this candle and starlit room, on a night of celebration and promise, stoops the Son of

God, on His knees, with a servant's towel wrapped around His waist and someone's dirty feet in His hands. He is in the position of a servant doing the task of a servant.

Yet He is the One who is in charge. This is clarified from the start – John observed that Jesus knew His Father had given Him all authority. It was in this moment His mission to wash feet. And that is precisely what He did. In spite of Peter's reluctance to cooperate and subsequent desire to have more than the others, Jesus washed only his feet. He served and He led.

Having finished His mission, Jesus returned the basin to the proper location, removed the towel, replaced His coat and turned to His disciples. To these stunned wannabe leaders Jesus said, "I've laid down a pattern for you. What I've done, you do. I'm only pointing out the obvious. A servant is not ranked above his master; an employee doesn't give orders to the employer. If you understand what I'm telling you, act like it – and live a blessed life" (Jn. 13:15-17 MSG).

This dramatic example provided a captivating climax to the way Jesus lived from day one. He had ceaselessly sought to make disciples using the simple strategy of a servant. He had led as a servant all through their three and a half years together. He had assigned them service roles as the way to lead in His Father's Kingdom. He modeled and developed servants who would affect others and, thus, leaders who were themselves, servants. However, it was not enough to know these things. If they were to be the kind of disciples who would one day be identified as the Bride of Christ it would be because they did what they knew to do. It would be because they expressed their identity as that of a servant, affecting the lives of others.

JUMBO SHRIMP, HALF FULL

The English language is complex. Take for instance, the *oxymoron*. By definition an oxymoron is a figure of speech in which contradictory ideas or terms are combined to create a brand new word or phrase. Even the word oxymoron is an example of this little language trickery. *Oxys* actually means sharp while *moros* means dull. Therefore, an oxymoron is a sharp dull (or is it a dull sharp?).

> *Almost exact.*
> *Soft rock.*
> *New classic.*
> *Freezer burn.*
> *Twelve ounce pound cake.*
> *Diet ice cream.*

Examples of oxymorons creep into popular language at an ever alarming rate. Phrases like 'jumbo shrimp' and 'half full' have been around for ages. Others are a little newer. When Adele and I dated, we were advised to avoid being 'alone together'. Growing up I sometimes found myself with friends who had been a bit mischievous. To avoid looking guilty they would tell me to simply 'act natural'.

Among the oxymorons that have been around the longest is the one introduced by Jesus in both example and command. It is the strategy He used to make disciples, the concept of servant leadership.

Servant leadership is two contradictory ideas that are held *at* the same time. We more often see people who play roles of servant or of leader, but not in concert. For example, a waiter might introduce himself to you by saying, "I will be your server this evening." Is this where he plans to spend his life? Probably not. He may be working his way through school or climbing the restaurant's corporate ladder. He may be your server tonight, but he is not in truth your servant. In fact, he is not really a servant at all. He is simply playing a role. He serves while he waits for the chance to lead, not because it is who he is.

His manager (a leader) may stop by your table during the meal to make certain that all is well. She too is playing a role. If a problem is uncovered (someone didn't do his job correctly), she slips from 'at your service,' to boss of the restaurant in order to intervene on your behalf and smooth over the situation. She will put on her manager's hat and sit with the waiter or cook who initially caused the problem. She serves out of role expectation, but never forgets her identity is leader.

Jesus, however, is a servant. That is how He affects change and guides people. He embodied these two very different notions in both identity and example. He modeled something very different than a person whose identity is leader but provides a service. He was able to avoid all of the positional, lord it over, jockeying for position ramblings that too often find their way into the local communities of faith called Church. And He hoped for His example to be our experience.

Another stirring picture of this path to disciple of Jesus can be found at the Galilean Sea Fish Grill. You'll find the story in John 21. In the story, Jesus is both owner/operator and chief servant for this seaside breakfast nook. He is creator of the world and all within it, including the sea and all those fish. Yet He chose as the best possible reflection of His own character, the role of servant. He arranged for the fire, the bread and the fish. When the disciples spotted the grill, none of them doubted that it was the LORD who arranged it... they were sure of it (verse 12). Immediately on the heels of observing that this was the LORD, John wrote, "Then Jesus served them ..." (John 21:13 NLT). Wow! The Master serving His people. Why? Because He was by nature a servant. It wasn't a role for Him to play. It was a matter of identity. I once heard someone say, "Servant leadership is not so much about what you do to serve. It is all about how you react when others treat you like a servant." Why would they treat you that way? Because it is who you *are*.

Paul was captured by this image of service as well. In his letter to the believers at Philippi he challenged them to consider Jesus' example. He wrote:

> You must have the same attitude that Christ Jesus had. Though he was God, he did not think of equality with God as something to cling to. Instead, he gave up his divine privileges; he took the humble position of a slave and was born as a human being. When he appeared in human form, he humbled himself in obedience to God and died a criminal's death on a cross. (Phil. 2:5-8 NLT)

The beautiful hymn of Jesus' humility and exaltation focused on His attitude. He made himself nothing. He humbled himself. These were visible actions that were preceded by and immersed in a servant attitude/heart. That is the attitude that we are to have.

A leader in this new Kingdom was not someone who had put in his or her time or earned the right to be called leader – to rise up to a certain position. A leader was not someone who exercised a lording authority over others, or acted as though he had the right to become a tyrant (Matt. 20:25-26). Instead, someone who led by affecting others (in God's Kingdom) recognized that he was one under authority... a servant. A leader trusted the

> **Servant leadership is not about a position – it is about an attitude – about heart.**

relationship s/he had with her/his authority. Such a servant affects people in his/her wake... this is how s/he leads. He or she would recognize that Kingdom leaders are in that role by assignment, not because they deserve it. Therefore the underlying attitude of the leader would be exactly the same as that of the servant. This is the key to servant leadership. Servant leadership is not about a position – it is about an attitude – about heart. It is not related to what you do. It is all tied up in who you are.

EMPLOYING DISCIPLES VERSUS ENROLLING DISCIPLES

A lot of churches have taken the journey of disciple making and framed it as a series of classes. For many of them spiritual development is a somewhat academic experience resting heavily on acquired knowledge and hoping for behavior or value change. The clarion call in such a model is, "Enroll now for our next class."

Jesus' example might cause us to consider adjusting that theme to "Employ now!" Mark 3:13f records the story of the selection of *The Twelve*. By that time there were crowds following Jesus. Among those in the crowd were a number that had become convinced (at some level) that He was indeed Messiah. Out of that undisclosed number we are told that He selected *The Twelve* who would be called apostles. He had earlier called these men to come and see for themselves, to follow Him, to become fishers of men, to be His disciples. Now He was calling them out from those who had accepted His invitation. He called them for three specific reasons.

First, they were called to be His regular, ongoing companions, *to be* WITH Him. Servant leadership, like much of Kingdom life, is better caught than taught. Jesus knew that. He was the one and only lesson they would likely access regarding this concept. His very life was the chief example of a servant attitude that affects others. This was not an attitude lesson they could learn from a book; not an attitude lesson they could learn from political, social, or corporate leaders. Truthfully, it was not an attitude lesson they were going to learn from most of their religious leaders. Servant leadership was not an action, a set of skills or behaviors. It was a passion buried deep in the soul. To live content to affect others by being a servant required a conviction that could be caught only if you were with Him, if you were His regular companion.

Second, He SENT out the disciples. To affect others as a servant also meant serving by appointment – as appointed. **That is what servants do... what they are told to do.** It is not, in truth, the servants themselves who affect those around them. Their influence, such that it is, is tied inseparably to *who they represent* in their service. Jesus was appointed to this work... it was His mission. He represented His Father in this. As His Bride, we are also appointed to the work – we are on His mission, with Him. We represent Him as we serve.

In the world around us, people serve while they wait for the chance to lead, or they serve because they believe themselves to be victims of some system, or they serve because it seems a way to earn a living with minimal responsibility. However, Jesus served because He knew it was THE way to deeply affect others. This conviction, little by little, spilled over to His disciples. As they grew to be, in heart/attitude, servants, they found themselves in the place and with the people to whom they were sent, simply and only by following Him. He knew where they needed to be. He knew with who they needed to be. How? Because He is a servant; serving His Father and His mission.

Third, these first disciples served at HIS PLEASURE. Because they were in reality servants who were appointed, they could represent Him with a kind of boldness. That is, when they served by His appointment, they pleased Him... they stood for Him... they spoke on His behalf. They served under His authority. It is important to note that the authority they received was of a Kingdom nature. They were not put in charge of the organizational structure of some institution. The authority was of a spiritual nature. This was not the kind of authority that accompanies position and power as the world counts power. The disciple making command is not given to an organization; it is given to an organism. In the second letter to the believers at Corinth, Paul wrote:

> We are human, but we don't wage war as humans do. We use God's mighty weapons, not worldly weapons, to knock down the strongholds of human reasoning and to destroy false arguments. We destroy every proud obstacle that keeps people from knowing God. We capture their rebellious thoughts and teach them to obey Christ.
> (2 Cor. 10:3-5 NLT)

The weapons Paul wrote about are spiritual in nature and require the direction of Jesus to be properly used. This ability to affect others for the Kingdom of God was freely given to His first disciples because they were with Him and sent out *by* Him... they were servants under His command.

Jesus did not enroll His first disciples in some kind of religious school. Instead, He employed them in His mission. They caught

His attitude, they did what He appointed for them, and they served at His pleasure. **This is what it is to be a servant who affects others → to own His attitude; to live as He appoints us; and to serve at His pleasure.** This is how we follow His example. I can find no reason to think that He has changed this strategy in our day.

As Selah grew to be one with Justus during this time of betrothal, she would adjust her attitudes and opinions to parallel his. It is called *submission*. It is incredibly *politically incorrect* in our day, but it was absolutely the world of the first century bride. Of course you might ask, why? Why would she do such a thing? The easy answer is because she absolutely knew that this special man was willing to sacrifice anything and everything for her. That made him the kind of person she would voluntarily choose to submit to.

As the Bride of Christ, we make that same freewill choice…to *submit* our lives to Him precisely because we know that He is the kind of Groom who has/will *sacrifice* it all just for us. This is how He affects us. It is how we affect others. It is the way we live when we are out and about. It is the way we engage each other within the family. At least one of our challenges as the Bride during this time of betrothal is to arrange life so that we actually *are* servants, expressing this way of being in such a spirit that others are affected and led to our Jesus. How? Read on.

CHAPTER 6
HIS EXAMPLE, *ours*
(A Practical Look)

THE 80/20 RULE AND THE CHURCH

Servant leadership is a great challenge for the Church today. While there are many theories as to why the Church, particularly the Western Church, specifically the American Church, has lost a handle on servant leadership, I think there is at least one reason. That reason is knotted up with secular business ideas popularly called the 80/20 rule (the Pareto principle).

According to this decades old rule, 20% of the people do 80% of the work. Twenty percent of the people give 80% of the time or money. This idea was born in the world of Italian economics, making a short jump to western industry models during the 1940's. It is influenced by a kind of employer/employee segregation that assumes employees work for what they can get out of the company. Therefore (logic concludes), the odds are good that the real contributions will be made by no more than 20% of the people. The other 80% will do as little as they can and ride the coattails of the truly devoted minority (at one time these were even called the trivial many). Those coattails may be financial or benefits in the area of time or other perks. But there is no real commitment, devotion, or loyalty to the company; only to the benefits of the company. The 20% are ultimately identified and promoted to management.

Having seen that law in action in society, the evangelical Church in America has merely bought into it as an irrefutable reality. The Church struggles to think of itself as an organism that is alive, the Bride of our Christ, with every part essential. Instead, we fall back to the idea that we are an organization and an institution. The Church has so adopted this law of industry that our structures actually support it, creating a self-fulfilling prophecy.

Consider this very typical example:

- Membership: around 200 (someone who has appropriately confessed their allegiance to Jesus and loyalty to the people who are this Church)

- Attendance: about 100 (many studies report that about 52% of members are missing in action)

- Assumption: 30 or so of the 100 are too young to serve in a position of ministry

- Service Positions: generally from 40 to 50 (which looks like half of the people attending)

- Duplication: a significant number of people will likely play 2 or more roles in any Church, for varieties of motives

- Conclusion: out of 200 people professing faith in Jesus (see membership), 30 – 40 different people may play a service or leadership role in the positional structure of the congregation – or about 20%

My experience would suggest that the best-oiled Church machines in the nation might create a 30/70 or maybe a 35/65 organization. Most, however, are not the best oiled of machines. Remember, Jesus' example in disciple making: **all disciples must serve** (and thus affect others). That means that the Church has bought – hook, line, and sinker – into a secular world model, leaving 65-80% of professed believers with no disciple building service to exercise... no way to express themselves as servant.

Rather than an 80/20 principle, the Kingdom requirement is a 100/100 strategy. That is, 100% of the people who know Jesus personally are making a contribution by being servants. In the first letter that Paul wrote to the Corinthian believers, he attempted to respond to some questions they had addressed to him. By the time we get to 1 Corinthians 12, we have arrived at their questions concerning spiritual gifts. In verse 12 of chapter 12 he compares the Body of Christ with the human body, observing that each has many parts but the many parts make up only one body. He uses an argument from the world of the absurd to point out that eyes, ears and noses do not exist alone. They are distinct parts, but they only live as a part of the whole. He then notes that this design of God for the human body is an excellent metaphor of his strategy for the Church (verse 18). He concludes this analogy by writing, "All of you together are Christ's body, and each of you is part of it" (1 Cor. 12:27 NLT). Quite simply, the biblical model is not for us to be satisfied with the 80/20 rule applied to the positions within the organization of our churches but it is to see the goal of 100/100: One hundred percent of the people who have the Holy Spirit of God living within them playing a Kingdom role through the life of the Church (the Bride of Christ). . 100% of the people involved; 100% serving to affect others.

> *Quite simply, the biblical model is not for us to be satisfied with the 80/20 rule applied to the positions within the organization of our churches but it is to see the goal of 100/100...*

This divine strategy creates a real challenge for the organizational Church, regardless of the model of Church that you employ. We will not be able to reach this goal with the positional system utilized in most churches. The Church as an organization develops tasks, jobs and job descriptions. Then we seek to fill those positions and thus accomplish those tasks. The organizational neatness of multiple positions requires skilled staff. We only need people to serve who have these specific skills: teachers who can teach, deacons who can deac, etc. **This leaves the typical Church searching for skill positions rather than servant leaders.**

The question begs to be asked, "How much skill does it take to wash feet?" Were there foot washing classes (Foot Washing 101) for which Jesus developed literature? Our enlightened ways of thinking have propelled us to take this wonderful exercise of service which so affected the lives of those men and structure it, organize it, create a positional leadership hierarchy, write job descriptions, define skill sets… exhausting. *As soon as a Church begins to think this way, service becomes about leadership and that becomes exclusive, leaving out an overwhelming number of people who are created and gifted to serve and affect others, but not skilled in the needs of a particular organization.* You are left to hope and pray for the day that the 80/20 rule becomes a reality for your people. You conclude that 80% of the people are living in some rebellion against God ***all because they do not fit your structures***. And in so doing, you *settle* for *potentially* discipling about 20% of the professed believers who call your Church their Church. Unacceptable.

I would not propose that churches engage in this process with some kind of malice. However, the truth haunts us at an almost imperceptible level that our structures and systems are not effectively making disciples. Thus, securing servants to keep the machinery up and going is resulting in a few positional leaders who are burned out rather than an army of disciples who are fired up.

HOW DID HE DO IT?

If it is true that Jesus used a 'we are servants who affect those around us' design to make the first disciples, providing that as the model for making all disciples, then how did He do it? How did He set out to involve 100% of the guys in 100% of the work of serving and thus make an impact?
He simply…

- did, while others watched;
- then did, while others helped;
- then helped, while others did;
- and finally, watched while others did.

First of all, He provided a seamless example. He behaved as servant affecting others while His disciples watched. Matthew 8:1-4 records one such example. A man, who had gone his whole life un-served by others, approached Jesus the Servant after a period of teaching. This bold step alone was at great risk to both the leper and to Jesus. Kneeling before Jesus he said, "If you want to, you can heal my body" (Matt. 8:2 MSG). This lowly and desperate leper was actually asking the Son of God to stop and serve him – to meet his need. A stunned crowd watched silently as Jesus reached out His hand and touched this untouchable man. As He touched him He said, "I want to. Be clean" (Matt. 8:3 MSG).

Did you see it? Jesus wanted to serve the leper. He chose to serve him. Having served this man, Jesus led him by giving a series of instructions. Serving, then leading; and His disciples watched the whole thing.

Secondly, He involved the disciples with Him. Or, He was servant and they helped. Matthew 15 includes the story of Jesus feeding four thousand men, plus women and children. Having healed and taught for three days, Jesus realized the lateness of the hour and the hunger of the crowd. Concerned that should they start home in this condition some might faint along the way, He collected the disciples for a pantry inventory. With only seven biscuits and a few small fish, Jesus began to serve. Step one: lead the disciples to gather the crowd into groups on the ground. Step two: thank God for His provision. Step three: give it to the disciples to distribute. If Jesus was able to take such a small amount and feed such a large crowd, He didn't really need the disciples to complete the task. But He chose them. He sent them out on His mission (the concern He had for the physical nourishment of the crowds). They had watched Him serve; now they helped Him serve.

Thirdly, the disciples served and led while Jesus helped. Matthew 17 provides an account of what we refer to as Transfiguration Mountain. While Jesus, Peter, James and John were on the mountain, the other disciples were busy in the valley. A man with a son possessed by an evil spirit came looking for Jesus. When the man and the boy found the other nine disciples, and realized that Jesus was not available, he asked them to help his son. They had seen Jesus serve people with similar needs. They had helped as He had served people with similar needs. Now, they stepped up to the plate, ready to serve as well. Months (or years) earlier, had someone afflicted with such an irrational and dangerous spirit approached any of these men (which was not likely to have happened), they would have been appalled, perhaps saddened, but probably would have chosen not to get involved. After seeing a new example and helping in similar acts of service, they tried to help. While they were unable to help, they tried. And, they learned a lesson about prayer and spiritual battles. Basically, they sought to serve and He intervened to help them.

Finally, the disciples served and led while Jesus watched. In John 4 we are told that Jesus watched as His disciples baptized others. In Matthew 10 we read of His sending them out in teams, on mission. Indeed, the whole of the book of Acts is a testimony to the effectiveness of the serving and leading of His disciples.

The example of Jesus leading/serving while the disciples watched; leading/serving while the disciples helped; the disciples leading/serving while Jesus helped; and the disciples leading/serving while Jesus watched are many. In fact, let me challenge you to lay this book down and take up your Bible for a while. Let your fingers do the walking through the four Gospels while you look at the occasions when Jesus served and how He affected others by doing so, at how He modeled and mentored servant leadership for His first disciples. What you will find is a plain and simple picture of the strategy He used to make disciples. Those disciples carried that same concept with them into the first Church. If we wish to be partners with Holy Spirit in making disciples of Jesus, we will do well to imitate His example – be servants who affect those around us.

SERVANTS WHEN WE ARE WITH THE FAMILY

"Because you're a member of this family. That's why!" And so ended my complaint diseur. One spring day in 1974 I went to bed an unemployed, underappreciated teenager and woke up a professional, customer service representative for the grocery industry. (Okay, I was a bag boy.) I had joined the ranks of the employed, out in the real world. I had others expecting me to pull my share of the load. I had school, homework, Church expectations, and a girlfriend. I was busy. But for reasons I failed to grasp until my own guys arrived at this same social milestone, my parents didn't seem to understand just how busy my life was. They continued to expect me to play roles around the house.

This strategy seems to be one most parents use without being taught. In spite of the fact that the kids are growing up and demonstrating their independence by taking on a job, there are still life lessons they need to learn at home. Those lessons, valued and woven into a lifestyle, will naturally play themselves out whenever they are away from home, but they are best learned in the safety of home. They are best taught by the people that God ideally designed to teach them – their parents. Parents are keenly aware that those lessons are not taught with a textbook in the living room. They are taught by serving. So the parents (sometimes using the unfortunate word chore) will say: "take out the garbage" or "clean up your room" or "have you done your laundry this week?" or "let me help you change the oil in your car."

As believers we live a good percentage of our lives out and about (away from home). However, lessons for living there are still best learned in the safety and security of home. These lessons are also learned, not by studying a textbook in a classroom, but by serving in real time and place. These lessons might well spill over into the marketplace, but they are still learned at home ... within the family of God, the Bride of Christ, His Church. They are learned as we serve one another in concrete ways.

Life lessons for the disciple of Jesus are also best taught by people who share the same DNA, the Spirit of Christ. A design for this model of learning and growing was given to us in the Bible. I think this is something of what God had in mind with spiritual gifts. The Holy Spirit, living within believers **is** the Gift of the Spirit. When He moves into the life of a believer, He brings supernatural enablings. These are the gifts of the Spirit. These gifts are not to individuals; they are to the Church, the covenant community of believers. To think otherwise is to think as a leader rather than as a servant... it is to think positionally. Those gifts to the Church are exercised – strengthened – each time we serve one another.

According to Paul in the fourth chapter of his letter to the churches at Ephesus, there were a few gifts given specifically to the Church to be exercised within the Church. The five spiritual gifts identified: apostles, prophets, evangelists, pastors, and teachers were given to equip the saints for their acts of service. Cultural bridge builders (apostles/missionaries), truth-tellers for God (prophets), Good News announcers (evangelists), shepherds to care and guide (pastors), and/or interpreters that connect Truth and life (teachers) **were given to equip the rest of us**. As the Bride of Christ builds bridges with those outside the culture of God's Kingdom, the apostle/missionary equips us. As we speak for God, the prophets help us. As we announce Good News the evangelists tutor us. As we care for and guide others, the shepherds give us an example to follow. As we connect Truth and life for others in our world, the teachers awaken us. These people equip as Jesus equipped, by example. **They were not given *to us* to do it *for us*, paid or otherwise.** As they serve in these ways, I watch, I help, and then they watch and help me. The result is a disciple of Jesus is born and grows.

These were not people of greater value – with a higher position. They were not holding positions at all; they were holding feet!

TAKE ME OUT TO THE BALL GAME

I am a huge baseball fan – the kind that knows way too many statistics about those who play the game. The kind that plans vacations around home schedules for teams all over the league. The kind that adjusts his personal schedule each Fall in order to watch the playoffs and the World Series. The kind that thinks there is no food like baseball stadium food. The kind that considers the 100-plus-days from the end of the Fall classic until the pitchers and catchers report for Spring training as the dark ages of sports in America. I am a serious fan of the game.

My favorite team is my hometown Baltimore Orioles (though I still pull for the team of my childhood, the Atlanta Braves). In spite of trades, injury lists, free agency, and farm club movement, I can likely tell you the names of 90% of the Orioles players. I also know who the coaches are. However, I must regretfully admit that I cannot remember the names of the trainers. You see them occasionally at a game. For example, if a player is injured in the game, one of the trainers will be the first to his side. Usually they need only take a look. Sometimes they spray some freezing solution on the injury so the player can continue painlessly. Once in a while they have to take the player off of the field for additional treatment. Before games they help players get loose. After games they help players heal. Between games they help players stay strong. I do not know their names → but the players do!

One of the images that has helped me to understand the equipping role of apostles, prophets, evangelists, pastors and teachers is this idea of trainer. Much like the sports fitness trainer, their task is to get the saints loose and ready for the game; to help the saints heal after a contest; to strengthen the saints in the in-between times; and to intervene at crisis moments during the game.

Can you imagine a baseball trainer who threatens to quit because his name is not listed in lights with the starting lineup? Yet, for the American Church, many of these equippers have gotten all confused about their role. In so doing they have deserted the attitude of servant, abandoned their assignment, and owned institutional structures that provide a form of authority that is no authority at all.

The equipper, like the trainer, understands the game and embraces his/her role for the cause. They know the contest is on the diamond, not in the clubhouse. They know the newspapers will report on the players, but the players will listen to the trainers. They know that, if they are ever to receive a world championship ring it will be because they have done their job, equipping the players to do theirs.

This, it seems to me, is a good picture of servant leadership within the family. Servants (trainers) equipping the saints (the players) to serve His mission in their world (out on the diamond). The Church must embrace the fact that the game is on the diamond (out in the world), not in the clubhouse (the gathered Church). Just like a family, we must learn *in the context* of real companionship, by serving and, thus, affecting each other. Then, we must carry these lessons out into our world. This is the way He made disciples. It should be the way we make disciples.

SERVANTS WHILE WE ARE OUT AND ABOUT

Through the years I have attended approximately 6,415 Church banquets. If every Church were to decide to stop hosting such events today, I am convinced 84.6% of chicken farmers would file bankruptcy tomorrow. Chicken (baked or fried); a green vegetable that vaguely resembles green beans; a starch (rice or potatoes) which stands proudly as an immovable lump in the center of the plate; a salad that has fallen limp from a *three hour tour* of the kitchen; a drink that was, at one time, instant tea; and a small bowl of sweet something make up the typical menu.

These events are often an institutional Thank You to some leader or group of leaders in the Church structure. During the announcements, the emcee of the evening will certainly say something like, "Before we go any further, I want Sister Kate and all her helpers in the kitchen to step out here for just a minute. Let's all show them how much we enjoyed the meal." And as if cue cards were unveiled in bright lights, everyone applauds enthusiastically. This is true in spite of the fact that everyone has indigestion. Why do we love to celebrate those who have served *us*? Why do we draw attention to those who serve within our structures?

Most churches have valued, structured and formalized how we serve one another in the family, to the degree that it is the only expression of what it is to be a servant. Many believe (consciously or subconsciously) that the people who hold certain positions within the Church family are the most important people *to* that Church. Because of this institutional value, we employ ministry experts whose job is to create enough positions for the largest number of people to serve in the Church. Over time most churches have excluded the out and about aspect of service altogether.

With our words we say, "You should be a servant of Jesus and a leader in His Kingdom throughout the week." But with our attitudes and actions we have failed to value the minister of auto sales, or the minister of public school teacher. We do not count the ministry of city bus driver, the ministry of policeman, or the ministry of department store salesperson. We do not equip anyone for any of these roles. We will never see 100% of the people involved in 100% of ministry if we keep thinking like this. And anyone not serving is someone not growing toward the image of Jesus.

As equipper Jesus worked with His disciples. As assigner, He sent them to those not yet convinced. He served a seeking leper, a hungry crowd and a dissatisfied father. He served questioning religious leaders and women with questionable reputations. He engaged His first disciples in serving the same kinds of people. He clearly valued being a servant within the family, but not as an end unto itself. Rather He saw it as a training center for the real

> ***Anyone not serving is someone not growing toward the image of Jesus!***

deal, happening out and about. He made disciples, pre-conversion and post conversion, the same way – as a Servant who affected peoples' lives. And He employed them to do likewise.

The Ephesians 4 text refers to the believers as 'the Saints.' In other passages we are told that **all** of these believers are also gifted for service and leadership. By serving, over time, they began to measure up to the full stature of Christ. In contrast to the equippers, the lion's share of their service (and subsequent impact) was expressed out and about (or to use the baseball analogy, on the diamond rather than in the clubhouse).

There was a season in the life of many churches when the topic of spiritual gifts was avoided at all costs. If you couldn't explain it, you just didn't bring it up. That day is no more. Unfortunately what has happened in many cases is no healthier than the former. It seems that the Church is so married to the idea of position and skill that we have actually made spiritual gifts all about our internal operational positions.

Many churches use spiritual gift inventories. These instruments are designed to help people have some idea of where to start their search for serving as God has wired them. New and improved tools now identify not only the gifts, but also the kinds of gifts that best match a variety of service opportunities, virtually all of which are defined as within the Church family. Most of these tools do not even consider service outside of the structures of the institutional Church. They really have little to do with understanding how God has wired us, and more to do with who might be the best choice to fill a position in the Church structures. In other words, they have become a human resources management tool designed to help people who will serve the organization to find greater satisfaction within the organization.

The result of this kind of thinking has been that many people now believe that if you have a certain spiritual gift you have the right to serve in some specific kind of office within the Church. (As I re-read that sentence I am struck by how far it is from the ideal of a servant attitude, appointed by Jesus, and serving at His pleasure.) This kind of thinking has made it impossible for the typical Church to experience the joy of seeing 100% of the believers engaged, within the family and out and about, in 100% of the service. It has also seriously skewed our understanding of what is the main task of those who serve within the Church family.

Servant leadership is a process that requires you to value the service of others, to submit to serve under their lead, and to affect others as you serve. It is a vision that is larger than family responsibilities (servants within the family), encompassing the broader Kingdom mission (servants when out and about). Servant leaders cast shadows of influence as they serve those around them. By serving, people continue to develop toward the full image of Jesus.

The best and most noble purpose for servants who lead can never be fully realized if all we do is enlist volunteers to staff our organization. Our focus must shift to helping individuals to grow into the increasing image of Jesus, affecting the world around them. This happens through a local Church, not just in a local Church. People who see themselves as leaders who provide a service become protective of those internal positions. This inevitably leads to our ancient and universal human wrestling match with selfishness, pride and power.

Servant leadership can never settle for measuring an individual's progress toward the likeness of Jesus somehow apart from the mission of Jesus. There is always an out and about concern. Servant leadership that is consumed by the institutional fabric of the Church is inconsistent with the mission that Jesus was on and has sent us on. As we serve within the family, we are learning life lessons that are demonstrated as we serve when out and about. We are equipped within the Church for the mission in the world. The great challenge is to streamline and focus how we serve within the family so that we have time, energy and resources to serve when we are out and about.

A SERVANT LEADER PARADIGM STORY

The seminary where I taught in Louisiana had a great variety of degree programs and support services, but nothing received as many oooos and *ahhhhhs* as the Child Development Center. Children from six weeks to school age filled the halls and the playgrounds of that building. Daily (weather permitting) field trips were taken around the whole campus. You might be exiting chapel only to have to stop for a stroller crossing. Or a line of four-year olds out for their daily stroll might interrupt your commute from one classroom to the next. Such was the case on one particularly hot day.

I do not remember his name. He was a real fireball: 100% four-year old boy and mischievous to the core. He kept his preschool teachers on their toes every hour he was present. Because of a handicap, his little legs were in braces and he walked with the aid of a walker. It was exactly the same tool you might see at a senior citizens center, only a miniature version. His handicap, however, did not slow him down.

One particularly oppressive day (any day between April and October could fit that bill in New Orleans), the teachers had kept the boundless energy of four-year olds cooped up inside a small room for far longer than one would think possible. In spite of the fact that the temperature was in the mid-90's, the humidity was in the low 90's, the heat index over 100, and the sun beating down, they decided to take the kids out for a brief stroll. Whenever the children walked around the campus they were attached to each other by a rope with carefully spaced handles. Each child held a handle, a teacher led the way and another teacher secured the rear. However, this little guy could not hold both the rope and his walker. The teachers had learned that placing him in the rear allowed him too much room to roam, so he followed the lead teacher.

The scene unfolded like this. The sun was shining, the steam was rising up off the cement sidewalks like a teapot in full boil, the kids were plodding along with rope in hand and the teachers were at the ends of their rope! This little guy pushed his walker so close to the heels of the lead teacher that from time to time, he pulled her shoe off. I don't know how long this lasted (I am told the teacher was unbelievably patient), but at some point the heat, the day, and the heel calluses pushed her over the deep end. She turned, and squatted in order to look him eye-to-eye. Then she asked with bottled up emotion, "What are you doing?" This little guy responded quite innocently, "Teacher, the sun is hot and I'm just trying to walk in your shadow."

This teacher was a servant leader by accident. We are commanded to serve and affect others with intention. She inadvertently cast a shadow for another to walk in as she served his need to get out and exercise. That service took place on the hot pavement – out in the real world.

Jesus served and led others that same way. It was His primary disciple making strategy. He employed them, if you will, to do as He had done, to be as He was. He equipped His disciples and provided gifts from His Spirit to ensure that such equipping would continue through His Church. But most of the servant leadership assignments were done when out and about, out on the hot pavement. That is where followers of Christ cast a shadow for others to walk in. Those tasks within the family are there to equip all of us for serving when we are out and about… to help us to grow up.

Many of our institutional structures too often lead to complexity, professionalism and skill requirements. Seeing the Church as the people, the beautiful Bride of Christ, a living organism, allows us to wrestle with the simple reality that growing toward Jesus and His likeness means serving, and in so doing, affecting people around us.

If we are as a Church to just embrace one, single identity – being disciples of Jesus who are making disciples of Jesus – we must ask, "How do we do that?" My suggestion is to follow His example. Classes and conferences are not inherently evil. Promotion and publicity are not always self serving. But Jesus did not design and distribute fliers to invite folks to His latest and greatest conference or class. He simply served, and because He was a Servant on mission, He affected everyone He touched. Along the way to expressing our new identity, one of the things we must do is become servants (like Him) and affect everyone we touch.

CHAPTER 7
HIS COMMUNITY, *ours*
(It's an *Image* Issue)

A TOUCHY-FEELY GUY LIVING IN A TECHNO WORLD

"Hello. My name is Randy and I don't understand technology." Cell phones make me crazy. I am your I.T. department's worst nightmare. I make the Amish look like Steve Jobs. While working on this project my computer crashed. The good news was that everything was backed up. The bad news was that no one could repair my computer (anyone know when they stopped servicing Windows 3.1?). Adele called computer centers all over the area. The conversation was very professional and very diagnostic right up until they asked about the brand of the computer. It was as if we had shouted a profanity during a silence retreat... like we had suddenly become unclean. Immediately the technicians changed from the good and helpful Dr. Jekyll to the evil Mr. Hyde. Short, choppy sentences ended with, "No help for you!"...computer Nazis!

As I was lamenting these circumstances for Jason, a computer guru rather than geek, he shared with me that many computer companies develop resources that are unique to them so that no one else can repair them and only they can replace them. This insight led to a discovery bigger than hardware – one that touched on the very DNA of the computer world.

Jason taught me that there were two basic philosophies at work in the computer industry. The one that I was most familiar with is called a Closed Source philosophy. According to this approach, software is developed by a very select group of people. Only the few understand how it works. The goal is a marketable product for users like me.

The success of the industry argues that there are advantages to such an approach. Decision making is generally faster because only a handful of people are involved. Controls are clearer so tampering with the product is limited (very important since users don't know how to correct something that has been tampered with and if they do, they don't have permission to do so).

I discovered that with a Closed Source product someone actually owns the intellectual property; they own the code. Confession Time: when I boot up a new software program I skim read all of the legalese that precedes the actual use of the resource, repeatedly and mindlessly clicking 'yes'. However, imbedded in that language is something called the EULA, or End Users License Agreement. When I click 'yes' to that, I am saying I understand that I don't own it (in spite of what I paid for it). I am just a licensed user.

The computer program is written in both computer language (digits) and a human language code. There is a lot of secretiveness. In the industry some refer to it as security through obscurity. The idea is that since only a few know how the program works, it is secure. As a user, you only get to interact with the software. You never own it, and in that sense, you never belong to that Closed Source network.

As I listened to Jason, I realized how uncomfortable I was with a lot of the concepts at work in a Closed Source philosophy. For example, I don't like being thought of as a user. I am uncomfortable that only a few are in the know. What if they fold? The secretiveness makes me wonder, "What are they hiding?" And since the whole strategy is market driven, I am never left satisfied. After all, if I were completely pleased with what I own (excuse me, what I am licensed to use), then there would be no need for me to buy the next upgrade that rolls off the line.

In contrast to this approach is the Open Source philosophy. According to this perspective, software programs are initially developed by any number of people, as few as one and up to thousands. These products are not fixed in time but are dynamic in nature. It is as if they are designed to evolve toward excellence (as opposed to replacing the product with the next generation). The focus is on the perpetual development of a product to be the best that it can be.

> **We want the surface benefits, but not the real value.**

In a Closed Source philosophy, the idea is to leave users hungry for the new bells and whistles in the next resource. In an Open Source approach, the goal is to involve the larger computer community in creating the new bells and whistles and fixing all of the bugs along the way.

Unlike the Closed Source model, an Open Source product (as the name implies) usually publishes the code, making it available for anyone to access. The support for a software program is not in the hands of a few that developed it, but in the hands of the many who own and use it. With an Open Source product, everyone in the community owns the resource, provided they respect both the program and the people.

To Love and to Cherish from This Day Forward

The Closed Source strategy exists and prospers because of people like me; people who are out of the loop and don't mind staying there; people who don't get it and, for whatever reason, have resolved that we never will. We are used by the industry, sometimes abused. We want the surface benefits but not the real value. The Closed Source approach allows us to remain passive. We do not need to get involved, to take ownership or to be responsible in any way.

On the other hand, an Open Source approach requires involvement. You must relate to the larger community. Solutions are found together. New applications are discovered with others. Anything you learn must be shared. After all, that is the responsible thing to do.

I am no longer writing about the computer industry. It occurs to me that the Church may have been the first to distinguish closed and open source approaches. So many churches have become Closed Source institutions. People on the outside are welcomed to our gatherings but few are actually allowed into the fabric of our lives. They may use our product, but the community is often for the few, the brave, the charter members. Our codes are internally understood but carefully secured from outsiders in the obscurity of our heritage and non-communicative language. Our systems are anything but dynamic. They are fixed in time and place. We permit a few, usually good intentioned, positional leaders to take custody of all of the responsibilities, allowing most to remain passive at best. This year's event must be bigger and better than last year's event, which was bigger and better than the previous year. Consumerism (not community) best describes our approach to the people of the world around us. They are prospective buyers of our product.

The beautiful Bride of Christ, the Church, on a quest to be healthy for her Groom, embraces her new identity and its complimentary task: to be disciples of Jesus who make disciples of Jesus. She adjusts life in order to follow Jesus' example: to be a servant who affects the lives of others. And, she knowingly fosters and protects the one and only atmosphere in which this way of living is possible, an Open Source atmosphere: community.

A COMMUNITY PRIMER

The Church is literally the bodily expression of the Kingdom of God in this world. It is (or should

> *An authentic Church strives for community and thrives because of community.*

be) a society that operates as God intended all along. We are after all a redeemed people, having been bought back and being brought back to God's original purpose. We have exchanged our birth citizenship for citizenship in the Kingdom of heaven. As such, we have the opportunity to model for the pre-Christian world what community could be like if it were not for separation from God.

Unfortunately the world watches our bickering, our divisions, our business sessions, hears our gossip, and concludes that a redeemed community is no better than an unredeemed community. This should not be the case. The Bride strives *for* community and thrives *because of* community.

Community was central in the first century Church and must become central in the twenty-first century Church. While community is simple, it is not easy. Social relationships or having friends is not the same as experiencing community. Joining a small group does not guarantee becoming a part of community.

Community is somewhat intangible. In the summer of 1999, in *Next*, Carol Childress of Leadership Network described it this way: "People can walk into the church [building] and sense something different. They feel the presence of God. They experience the vitality and spiritual dynamic present. Even visitors recognize it." Did you notice the words? *Sense something. Feel. Experience the vitality and spiritual dynamic. Recognize it.* The article continued, "Authentic community, of all the characteristics of the twenty-first century churches, is perhaps the hardest to describe because it is a by-product, an outflow of the health and vitality of the congregation." Defining community is a little like finding salt in a pecan pie. **You don't taste it when it's there, but you do taste it when it's not.**

Community is all about relationships. A debate rages in some evangelical circles concerning the front door into the Church. Some believe the front door is the public worship event. The advocates of this view argue for greater seeker sensitivity, for higher quality, for timely delivery and mass marketing. Others contend that the front door is actually the smaller group (Sunday School class, Bible study group, cell group). They say people desire greater intimacy and are therefore attracted to these types of settings. **It seems to me that the front door into the Church has not changed in 2000 years - - it was and is relationship.** As believers in Jesus Christ meet and build authentic relationships with pre-Christians, they personalize and validate the faith. They introduce these not yet family members to their Christian friends and invite them to worship events and smaller group experiences. At each step they are expanding the community base for the nonbeliever until a great cloud of witnesses surrounds the seeker. In this environment the Holy Spirit does some of His best work.

The western world in general and America in particular have become a series of disconnects. The population is transient; increasingly smaller numbers of people live near extended family; work associates are seen as competitors; loyalty no longer exists - not to this job, this product, this neighborhood, or this spouse. This sense of being disconnected from others (or only virtually connected through the mushrooming world of social networks) has created a real hunger within many people for a sense of belonging to another ... a desire for community.

> **Then the LORD God said, "It is not good for the man to be alone." (Gen. 2:18 NLT)**

In this respect, community reflects a hole in the heart of the pre-Christian, demonstrating the importance of community to the work of the Church when she is out and about. Within the Body of Christ, real growth in the faith can only happen in an honest and trusting environment. In that environment confession can lead to healing. Honesty can cultivate integrity. Transparency can repair relationships. Accountability can foster holiness. In many ways, it is the same as the healthy growth of any individual. That is, health and growth best occur in the family setting where honesty and trust prevail. That kind of environment is what I am describing as community.

THE BIBLE AND COMMUNITY

The story of the Bible is one of community – created, lost, and reestablished. Creation includes the coordinated work of God: Father, Son and Holy Spirit, in what Gil Bilezikian has called an eternal community-of-oneness (*Community 101* by Bilezikian 15f). John Ortberg has described God as a community engaged in an eternal, divine dance (*Everybody's Normal Till You Get To Know Them* by Ortberg 34-35). The Bible introduces the notion this way, "Then God said, 'Let us make human beings in our image, to be like ourselves'" (Genesis 1:26 NLT). Having created man, singularly, God made the remarkable declaration, "It is *not* good...." This was the one and only time in creation that God identified something as not good. However, He did not leave us hanging as to what the not good element was. The Scripture records it this way: "Then the LORD God said, 'It is not good for the man to be alone'..." (Genesis 2:18 NLT). The creation of a companion completed creation, fixing the not good.

God set out to create a being in His own image. This, however, seemed impossible when the creation was only one because only one is not a community. So in Genesis 2:18f we are told of the creation of the woman, a companion. Dr. Bilezikian and others have noted that the Hebrew word translated as helper or helpmeet could well refer to, "A rescuer from this state of affairs" (*Community 101* 20). With this rendering, the creation of a woman rescued man from the state of being alone. She is not a divinely given assistant. Rather, she completes the image of God in His crowning work of creation: people. These two were indispensable to one another. Without each other the possibility of community simply did not exist and therefore, the image of God was somehow mysteriously missing.

As long as the man and woman were in right relationship with God, they were in oneness together. However, the moment that they broke their communion with God, they discovered that their own relationship had broken down. All of the ingredients necessary for community with one another and the actual experience of the image of God (things like honesty, trust and respect) were lost when relationship with God was abandoned.

In light of this, it seems altogether appropriate to refer to Genesis 3 as *The Fall*. By the time we arrive in chapter 4, people are killing one another. In Genesis 6 God appears remorseful for ever creating humanity. By Genesis 11 the selfish desire to regain the image of God reaches a crescendo as people determine to build a tower to reach the heavens, an attempt to have community with God, but from impure hearts. The result of the effort was the confusion of tongues, breaking down communication. Where there is no communication there is no community. Much of the rest of the story of the Old Covenant is one of the failures of His people to achieve community and God's unending stash of second chances.

God continued to demonstrate His desire for relationship and community by initiating a covenant with Abram and renewing it with Isaac and then with Jacob. Through Moses, God sent the law. Paul was the first early Christian actually to pen down his own wrestling match with the purpose of the law. He indicated that God gave the law in order to show people their own inability to deserve or earn community with Him (Rom. 7:7-13).

God, it seems, ceaselessly desired a people who would be His priests to the nations; a people with whom He could enjoy community and through whom He could reestablish community with others. According to Galatians 4:4, at just the right time, when everything was in place, God sent His Son into the world, not to condemn the world for failing to rebuild community without Him, but to once and for all offer community with Him and with each other.

Jesus modeled the pattern of community for His followers. Early in His ministry we are told that He selected twelve of His followers to "accompany him" (Mk. 3:14 NLT). He sought to build relationships with His closest associates, His best friends, the hungry seekers who surrounded Him, and even people who represented His enemies. Henry Blackaby, in *Experiencing God*, described this unending pilgrimage of God this way: "God pursues a continuing love relationship with you that is real and personal" (42f). That is, God desires to reestablish community with us and between us.

HOW FAR WE HAVE COME

Linguistic experts tell us we are what we say. I remember an experiment where a teacher had filled a dark glass with an unknown liquid. He asked us, "Do you know what is in the glass?" The brainstorm resulted in a long list of possibilities. He then placed the glass on a table and began to pound his fists on the table, careful not to touch the glass. As he pounded, the table trembled. As the table trembled the liquid in the glass changed from a quiet pond to a turbulent sea, spilling over onto the table. His point was if you want to know what is inside the glass, shake things up around it because whatever is inside is what will spill out. From that illustration he observed that our language is much the same way. Whatever is inside us is what spills out whenever we speak.

It has been called Zioneese, Christianeese, The Language of Zion, and Church Talk. Everyone understands that it exists but few are willing to tackle translating it for the masses. More than the problem of words that are nonsense to the culture around the Church, there is the bigger issue of using simple words but communicating a distorted message. One example of that has to do with community. American Church talk is filled with questions like these: "Did **you** have **your** quiet time today?" "Have **you** provided a personal witness today?" "How did **you** respond to worship today?" "Did **you** read **your** Bible today?" "What is going on in **your** life?" Everything, it would seem, is centered on the individual.

In contrast, New Testament Church talk is altogether different. For example:

> ...we all belong to **each other** (Rom. 12:5 NLT)

> Love **each other** with genuine affection, and take delight in honoring **each other** (Rom. 12:10 NLT)

> Live in harmony with **each other** (Rom. 12:16 NLT)

> For you have been called to live in freedom... freedom to serve **one another** in love (Gal. 5:13 NLT)

> Be patient with **each other**, making allowance for **each other**'s faults because of your love (Eph. 4:2 NLT)

> ...be kind to **each other**, tencerhearted, forgiving **one another**, just as God through Christ has forgiven you (Eph. 4:32 NLT)

> And further, submit to **one another** out of reverence for Christ (Eph. 5:21 NLT)

> Don't lie to **each other** ... (Ccl. 3:9 NLT)

> Make allowance for **each other**'s faults, and forgive anyone who offends you (Col. 3:13 NLT)

> Teach and counsel **each other**... (Col. 3:16 NLT)

So encourage **each other** and build **each other** up...
(1 Thess. 5:11 NLT)

You must warn **each other**... (Heb. 3:13 NLT)

...think of ways to motivate **one another** to acts of love and good works (Heb. 10:24 NLT)

This short survey of Scripture demonstrates the deep contrast between the way the Bible describes the life of faith and the way contemporary Church life explains the same. We think of Christianity in the singular with community implications. This deep conviction spills out from us through the words that we use. We run to the closet of isolation rather than the small group of community with our weaknesses, failures, and successes. The Bible, on the other hand, presents a Christian faith that is communal with personal implications. That is true in the grand opening of the Bible. Though lost in *The Fall*, the possibility of community is restored in the sacrifice of Jesus. The experience of community in this life is now possible due to grace and mercy.

> **The experience of true community is the proverbial upstream swim against culture, even against the prevailing Church culture.**

The question must be raised, "If community is so critical to what it is to be Christian, why has the contemporary Church shied away from it?" There are many barriers to the experience of community among a covenanted group of followers of Christ. There is the Judas barrier: the possibility always exists that we will embrace someone who ultimately disappoints us and, in so doing, may bring painful consequences to all. There is the Martha barrier: people are busy and distracted (many times

To Love and to Cherish from This Day Forward

they are busy because the Church schedule has left them that way) and community takes time.

Pride, an ancient and universal condition, hampers our very best efforts to be real, honest and transparent with one another. The high value placed on rugged individualism (the Jack Bauer Syndrome, or the disease of the self made man or woman) leaves generations thinking that to recognize we were made for community is an admission of weakness. The experience of true community is the upstream swim against a powerful culture, even against prevailing Church culture.

So is community worth the effort? Jesus thought so. His first followers championed it. The Bride of Christ throughout the ages has constantly hungered for it. The persecuted Church in our world today hangs on by means of it. And that aching hole in our own hearts yearns deeply for it. To be in a place, among a people, where I can be the self I brought into the family and become the self that the Groom always had in mind. That is certainly worth the effort.

During her betrothal, Selah embraced and expressed a new community. She discovered new cousins, uncles, aunts, brothers, sisters, moms and dads. She was immersed into a new system of traditions as well as familiar ways with new twists. She also learned to express this new place of belonging not only with her new family, but when she was out and about, to the people who had known her for years and the new people she met on the street. Her new identity included a new family and new implications for friendships.

The development of this new sense of community was hard work for Selah, calling for new ways of thinking and being. Community is hard work for us as well. It is an expression of the very image of our good God, bought for us at great cost to

Him. It is recognizable to anyone who has ever experienced it, and clearly evident in its absence. And it is woefully missing in most churches in our day... churches that have become content with a cheap imitation in the form of distant acquaintances. Like the other characteristics of a healthy Bride of Christ, community has a way of expressing itself within the family, as we relate to each other, and when we are out and about, as we engage a watching world. We will explore these in the next chapter.

CHAPTER 8
HIS COMMUNITY, *ours*
(Deep Fellowship and Real Friendship)

Now that we know community is a God characteristic... something He built into the original design... something He so desires for His Son's Bride that He paid dearly to reclaim it for her, it is important to consider what community might look like. This is the environment in which the Church matures toward all she can be. Let's think a bit about how that looks as we engage each other and as we encounter those yet to embrace the Jesus who is changing us.

COMMUNITY WHEN WE ARE WITH THE FAMILY

What does community look like within the Body of Christ? The word that is most often used is fellowship, or *koinonia*. Henry Blackaby has defined *koinonia* as, "... the fullest possible partnership and fellowship with God and with other believers" (*Experiencing God* 193). The emphasis here is on a kind of partnership. I am a simpleton, so the easiest way for me to define fellowship is: two fellas on a ship. Let me explain.

The city of New Orleans has been nicknamed the Crescent City by people who first noticed that the mighty Mississippi River forms a crescent around what is now the central business district of the city. Generally speaking, the Mississippi River runs northwest to southeast between Baton Rouge and the Gulf of Mexico. A ship going down stream would be sailing in that direction. However, around the city of New Orleans, in order to go from northwest to southeast, you will briefly sail south, southwest, east, north, northeast and east again. Everyone on the ship will sail in all of those directions each time the ship turns.

The most frequent guests on the Mississippi River around the city are huge cargo and tanker ships. These giant vessels tower several stories up from the surface of the water when they are empty, riding high in the river. However, when they are loaded, they ride so low in the water that someone watching from the shore has to wonder how they keep from going under. When the ship is high in the water, everyone on board is high in the water. When the ship is low in the water, everyone is riding low as well.

This, to me, is the essence of what fellowship is all about. It is a keen awareness, experienced daily, that I am not traveling this spiritual journey alone. Indeed, I am covenanted to a number of shipmates, those partners who are my Church. We sail together in the same direction, turning together, fighting the current together, drifting with the current together, riding high together and riding low together.

> *We maintain formal, professional, sterile, distanced, social acquaintances with the very people with whom we were remade to share community!*

Fellowship is a level of relationship reserved for believers only. While we can and must have friends among the not yet converted, we can experience fellowship only with those who share our partnership with God through Jesus Christ. Unfortunately, the vast majority of relationships within the Church are a mile wide and an inch deep. We maintain formal, professional, sterile, distanced, social acquaintances with the very people with whom we were remade to share community. We have done this for so long that the aching desire for community, which still exists within most of us, has been suppressed by the deception that acquaintances are the best we can expect or experience prior to eternity.

That was not the case with the first Church and it need not be so with us. Fellowship had several significant characteristics among the first followers of Christ that are transferable to any culture and any style of Church, including your own.

Shared Life

By shared life, I refer to the natural consequence of true fellowship, of community in the Body of Christ. Read Acts 2:43-47. Notice the shared life components sprinkled throughout the text . . .

- They shared the celebration and awe associated with miraculous signs and wonders.

- They met together, which is, of course, not the same as having a meeting.

- They shared everything they had with other believers.

- They sold their possessions and shared the proceeds with those in need.

- They worshiped together, and this was not an event they attended, but a life of worship they led.

- They met in homes for the LORD's Supper, constantly reminding each other of the One and Only who united them.

- They shared their meals with great joy and generosity, not as social acquaintances, but as a family feast.
- They shared in the community favor, not that everyone agreed with them, but anyone who knew them was impressed by their devotion.

The life lived by the believers in the first century was not the isolated life of a lone ranger, but the communal life of a people surrounded by true partners in the journey of faith. It was not a life of lonely introspection, but a shared life.

Accountability

Accountability is a characteristic of community that is talked about much, but experienced very little. It is a concept that is often misunderstood in our culture. I would say that we frequently confuse accountability with Church discipline. Discipline happens after a fall. More times than not, we act confused and shocked that sin has occurred. Sometimes a biblical reclamation effort is made. Many times our own shame and embarrassment over what has happened drives us to act without being redemptive at all. The truth is, Church discipline doesn't really happen that much anymore.

> *Accountability is a wonderful preemptive strike against sin with a recovery plan pending.*

However, accountability is a wonderful preemptive strike against sin with a recovery plan pending. It is preemptive in that you have one, two, maybe three people, perhaps from within your small group. Those people are the people with whom you are most open and honest.

The writer of the book of Hebrews challenged the first century Church to "...strip off every weight that slows us down, especially the sin that so easily trips us up" (Heb. 12:1 NLT). This is the place where true accountability intersects the spiritual journey. It is important to remember that the writer was addressing people who were faith convinced that Jesus is God's One and Only answer to the needs of the world. He is not writing to pre-Christians. It stands to reason that he is not addressing the *condition* of sin, but he is talking about those specific sins that so easily hinder our progress toward the experience of Jesus' image in and through us moment by moment.

It is not necessary to ask what that sin is because everyone reading this book already knows you have a sin or two with which you struggle. The enemy has a way of finding that place that is our weakest point and tempting us there from time to time. Accountability exists when a group of believers engaged in real life are willing to be authentic with each other. That authenticity includes the courage to say to each other, "This is a problem for me." Since it is the God given desire of those who are converted to want to become increasingly like Jesus and the natural result of community to admit that we need each other's help to get there, we agree to accountability. Needing someone to discipline us after we have sinned is not the critical issue. We need someone to be available to help us when we are being tempted.

> *I need someone that I can call and say, "HELP" when I need help!*

I need as a growing believer to know that there is somebody in my spiritual family, someone with whom I have been so authentic, so honest, and so transparent about the sin that entangles me, that I can call and say, "HELP" when I need help. Such a relationship is imperative if I am going to be perfecting toward the image of Jesus.

The sad truth is, I will disappoint God, myself, and others from time to time. When that happens, I will need someone to discipline me, to dust me off, to love me, and to get me going again. But I really need somebody to keep me from falling so often. The bruises add up over a lifetime and leave my ability to witness weakened. I have Holy Spirit living within me. Every believer does. He is empowering me for the Christ life. But I need somebody to hold me accountable for follow through.

Accountability is a wonderful, positive, proactive, preemptive strike against the enemy. Jesus held His disciples accountable. He built an accountability (partnership) system into service leadership assignments. After His ascension, they immediately elected a new apostle, so no one was without a partner. The first Church seemed to lovingly recreate this dynamic as small groups of believers met in homes to share life on a daily basis. The story of Ananias and Sapphira, recorded by Dr. Luke in Acts 5, demonstrates the seriousness of the Church when it came to sin. But the underlying question of that story for me is, "How, with the Church expanding so fast, was it not repeated over and over again?" The answer, I think, is simple: a community that acted like a real family, holding each other accountable.

COMMUNITY WHILE WE ARE OUT AND ABOUT

My first real best friend was Barry. We met in the seventh grade and had only two things in common. We both played saxophone in the band (a real chick magnet) and we both had unique (some would say twisted) senses of humor. Those were the days when a weird sense of humor was not vulgar, just different. Apart from each other, the humor was only average. But when we got together, we sharpened each other.

By eighth grade we had moved past joke telling in the cafeteria to writing and performing (albeit, just for friends and as class projects) a variety of skits. By ninth grade we had written a full length, tongue-in-cheek play. Then, thanks to the Georgia Public School System and at the encouragement of every faculty member from our junior high school, we were separated for high school. Our friendship continues but our captive audiences are gone.

During our years together Barry came to know and love Jesus and challenged me to grow in my walk of faith. We ended up in the same Church for a part of our youth. He was best man for my wedding. I was honored to perform the ceremony when he and his wife, Shirley, married. Now, many years later, we see each other on very rare occasions. Thanks to the e-world, we have exchanged an infrequent email or two and watch from a distance via Facebook. But whenever I hear his voice on the phone, my load lightens and I smile. I know, should anything happen, he is among the handful of people that I could call at the drop of a hat. Regardless of how long it has been, he would intervene to help. He was and is my friend. Until seventh grade, I had a lot of neighborhood and school acquaintances. But Barry taught me what friendship was all about.

Jesus had many critics. The criticism came from government officials, positional religious leadership and the average Joe on the street. Some of the criticism was born out of jealousy or envy. Other criticism was rooted in racial prejudice. Much criticism came from those who were ignorant – those who never met Him or got to know Him. Even His own family was painted with various degrees of skepticism about Him. With such an assortment of opposition, you would think the criticism would have been just as varied. However, that was not the case. Two themes appeared over and over again from those who struggled with this Galilean carpenter's claim of Messiahship. What concerned Jesus' critics most was His claim to be the Son of God and His choice of friends.

In the quiet recesses of my mind, I often wonder if many of today's churches (the Bride of Christ) would be accused by our neighbors as living as though God is our Divine Parent or having friends who are far from Him. Most convicting is the thought that those around *me* might not make those accusations either. The neighbors around the people who are the

> ***We call them prospects, but Jesus called them friends.***

Church often perceive us to be yet another good, social institution, representing one of many competing belief systems that help people survive life and cope with the inevitability of death. They recognize our valuable contribution to society. They see our buildings as branch offices and hope that we are able to help them raise their property value. They recognize our potential economic value to the neighborhood. But I wonder, do they see us as the children of God, the ambassadors of a Kingdom that is real? Do they see in us the image of their Creator? Do they see us as friends?

A great part of the problem is our failure to be their friends. They simply do not know us. And more often than not that is because we do not know them. We drive past them as we go to gather with the Church for worship. We sit in a cubicle near them at the office. We stand and cheer for our favorite team in a stadium filled with them. We call them prospects, but Jesus called them friends.

> **We remember that we have an enemy...that's good. But we start to think that pre-Christians are it!**

As we are out and about interacting with the world around us, community is experienced as legitimate friendships with people who are not yet convinced. If you choose to build such friendships, you run the risk of hearing the same kinds of cutting comments that Jesus heard from religious people in His day. In spite of the risks, He persisted. The truth is there are numerous rational reasons why believers should not have close friendships with pre-Christians. However, I can think of one good reason to be friends with them. He was, and we are to be like Him.

Most of the Church (the Bride of Christ) are not good at developing friendships, even within the Body of Christ. That causes challenges when we try to move to become friends with those still seeking. For example, many churches have adopted the mantra: we are a friendly Church. As many others have said, the problem is that pre-Christians are not searching for a friendly Church. Check with them. They'll confirm it! They are, however, searching for friends. In spite of the fact that our deepest desire is for these people to defect from the kingdom of this world, into the kingdom of God, we create a competitive kind of environment that often prevents the development of real friendship. They are on one side and we are on the other. We remember that we have an enemy; that's good. But, we start to think that pre-Christians are it.

Another challenge we face with building friendships with unbelievers is that the only place to which we seem to invite them is a Church building. Indeed, because so many of us are at the Church building in every free moment, that is the only place they can actually come to see us. Many of our Church schedules have even programmed outreach. If you want to reach pre-Christians, you must come to the Church building on a certain night of the week and go out into the dark with a card you cannot read to see a person you do not know at a place to which you have not been invited. Staying home and having pre-Christian friends over does not count. In fact, many reaching systems even discount such a decision, wondering why you were not devoted enough to go to outreach night.

Smaller groups are a great way to expand the friendship base for those who do not yet know God. Yet many such groups operate on the "only Christians allowed" model. Changing this paradigm will be yet another barrier to overcome in building friendships with pre-Christians. Smaller groups can and should grow because of marketplace relationships (rather than expecting the Church as institution to assign new members to a group). Friendship evangelism, or what Jim Petersen has called affirmation evangelism (Living Proof 83f), depends on

> *The truth is, very many people never hear the message of Christ because the message of our own lives is so loud...*

friendship building all the time we are out and about. Then those real friends are invited to informal, cozy settings to explore matters of faith with a small group of journeyers. Friendship with sinners (community while we are out and about) has to do with letting a seeking person see what a redeemed community looks like and feels like up close: not perfect, but redeemed. It is to let them into our community, even before they are fully convinced of the foundation of our community. Why? Because if they come and see Him in us; they are much more likely to be attracted to Him.

Another bridge to cross in moving to genuine friendship building with pre-Christians is the bridge of attitude. Those of us who are believers are so saddened by the fact that so many people actually choose to reject Jesus. We are stunned that anyone could refuse so great an offer. In order to deal with that disappointment, we build attitude walls. Often those walls help us to cope by saying things like, "I am not surprised. We are told that the preaching of the cross will be offensive." Walls, however, always mean barriers. Sometimes we use such thinking as a permission slip to go ahead and offend people ourselves. Many well intentioned believers have forgotten that it is the preaching of the cross (the message itself), not the preacher (or the messenger) who is to be offensive. The truth is, very many people never hear the message of Christ because the message of our own lives is so loud, or because they do not know us. It is important to remember that He was not offensive. In fact, just the opposite was true. He attracted all sorts of people of unsorted reputations. It was His message that caused them to leave.

I once read a statistic that claimed there is a better than 50% chance that someone who is invited by a real friend to a worship event or small group gathering will say, "Yes." I don't know the source or how accurate that statistic is. In my own life, I would say it is better than true. **When a friend asks me over, I am inclined to say yes unless I find I simply cannot go. When a stranger invites me somewhere, I am inclined to say no unless I find I simply cannot get out of it.**

True or not, just imagine the possibility that one out of every two unchurched people with whom you are friends would likely respond to an invitation to investigate Christ if you asked. Now multiply that by the number of believers who are currently a part of your Church family. The possibilities are staggering. But it means that we have to be their friend. We have to move from front door, bell ringers to back door guests in the homes of people who may be far from God.

There is one more component to this idea of community, expressed when we are out and about. Acts 2 provides a multi-faceted snapshot of life in the first Church. The closing verses of that text describe a group of people who are literally sharing life together as they patiently and persistently announce great news throughout their town. The problem of course is that not everyone in town recognizes the news as great. For them to accept that message seems to mean that they will have to reject much of what they have been taught and thought their whole lives. Persecution for these messengers of God's Good News is all around them. Initially it is ridicule, but quickly it deteriorates to family expulsion, rejection by lifelong friends, loss of job, loss of home, and ultimately loss of life. In this setting an incredible description is given, "...and enjoying the goodwill of all the people" (Acts 2:47 NLT). All of the people? In a town where ridicule and rejection abounds? In a setting where doctrinal disagreement resulted in the crucifixion? In that place, at that time, those followers of Christ enjoyed the goodwill of all the people? How so?

An initial reading of that text could lead one to conclude that everyone jumped on board the Jesus Bandwagon. However, the rest of the story tells us otherwise. While many people came to accept Jesus as Messiah and LORD, the overwhelming majority of the population did not. So what happened here?

I can only speculate at this point. Imagine you are sitting at home in your favorite chair, with an ice cold soft drink, a warm piece of fresh, homemade pie and the television remote which you are using to surf the airwaves. As you peruse the options for the night, you stumble across a commercial. Normally, that's a no brainer. You pass on by. But this catches your attention. It is almost like a Hallmark movie reduced to a one minute spot. You are captured by the scenery, engaged by the dialog and caught up in the short story. Then at the very end you find that the commercial is promoting a religious cause that you consider to be cultic. You sit back and might offer a commentary something like this: " cannot agree with those people, but I do admire their devotion."

This I think is at least included in what is meant by that phrase, *enjoying the goodwill of all the people*. The majority of the residents were not inclined to accept the message. Many cast family members and friends out of their circle of influence because of the message. Many

> **Even when people disagree with our message, do they still find themselves wanting the life that they see us live together?**

employers likely fired employees who chose to follow Christ. Yet the coffee shop commentary must have gone something like this. "I'll tell you what. I thought when I fired him for his faith he would recognize his mistake and come back on bended knee. But I heard that Barnabas sold some of his land and took a portion of the money to set up a fund for their family. Their needs have been met and they continue in their mission." Or "I thought when I threw her out on the streets, she would change her tune. Instead, one of their families has taken her in and now she's a part of their lives." Every conversation must have ended with something like, "I can't agree with those people, but I do admire their devotion. They are real. They are genuine. This is not a game to them. I'd like to have a passion like that!"

This testimony of community lived before a watching world compels me to ask: "What about your Church?" "What about my Church?" Remember, the Church is not an institution. It is a people. I am not asking what marketable front we promote to our neighbors. I am asking what do people in your neighborhood whisper at the grocery store about the people who are your Church? Do the people of God who covenant together to form your local Church have a good reputation in the neighborhood or at work? When people disagree with our message, do they still find themselves wanting the life that they see us live together?

A sense of community expressed when we are out and about means that we learn to take seriously Jesus' prayer for us: "I'm not asking you to take them out of the world, but to keep them safe from the evil one… Just as you sent me into the world, I am sending them into the world" (Jn. 17:15, 18 NLT). Authentic Church – the real deal – will always equip people to build genuine relationships with people who do not yet know Jesus, give them time to do it, and hold them protectively within it. Such a Church recognizes that the experience of community is potentially the greatest strength of our witness to those still seeking, or the greatest deterrent to their coming to Christ.

BISCUITS, DISCIPLE MAKING AND COMMUNITY

I love homemade buttermilk biscuits. I don't care much for the kind of biscuits that are scratched out of a can and shaped like a coaster. Adele and I spend a lot of our best couple time in the kitchen and biscuits are one of the things we like to bake.

Biscuit making is more than a science. There is an art to it. You begin by cutting butter into flour, sugar, and baking soda. A cookbook can tell you what it ought to look like, but you have to see the texture and learn the feel of the crumbs between your fingers in order to get it right.

After the flour and butter are just the right texture, you add the buttermilk. Now this is about the only thing that buttermilk is good for; you can bake with it. You want to avoid taking a big swig of buttermilk at all costs (I speak from experience). You mix the buttermilk in with the flour and butter. Once again, this has to be done incrementally (it's all in the wrist).

Next, take a piece of waxed paper and lay it out on the counter. Be sure to put a little water on the counter so the paper doesn't move around during the next step. And be certain to sprinkle some flour on the paper so the dough doesn't stick. Dump the dough onto the flour sprinkled, water secured, waxed paper surface and begin to knead appropriately. (For those who do not watch the Food Network, that means you flour your hands and pat the dough pile with a little more flour, then fold it gently until the dough is stiff and not sticky.) Too little or too much kneading will not a biscuit make.

After kneading, you roll out the dough. At my house, the rolling process results in something of an incline. That is for a very good reason. Adele likes big, thick biscuits and I like the thin and crispy kind. Then you take your favorite glass, which is the perfect size for a biscuit, and you put a little flour on the rim of the glass and begin to cut out the biscuits. We have concluded that the better way to bake biscuits is in a cast iron skillet, so that is where we lay the freshly cut dough next to each other.

It would be silly at this point to stand back, look at the perfectly round dough pieces laid next to each other in a room temperature iron skillet and conclude, "Viola! We have made biscuits." While we do have the right ingredients in the right amount and in the right order, we do not have biscuits. In order to turn appropriately prepared dough into melt-in-your-mouth buttermilk biscuits, you need the right environment, an oven set on 450 degrees, for 10 to 12 minutes.

When people begin a spiritual journey toward an encounter with Jesus and the expression of His likeness, their lives might well be filled with all the right ingredients, in the right order and just the right amount. However, they cannot adequately travel that journey without the right environment – the environment that they should have come to enjoy as friendship while they searched and they should come to discover as fellowship once they are in the family. The environment in which disciples are made is the atmosphere of community... not something experienced alone or in a crowd, but in a spiritual family where everyone serves and affects the lives of others. This is where disciples of Jesus rise up, mature; it is where they are made.

CHAPTER 9
HIS AUTHORITY, *ours*
(Making Decisions by Discerning and Submitting)

WHO IS IN CHARGE AROUND HERE?

The giant old tree had stood there next to the rural, Kentucky parsonage for as long as anyone could remember. It was a great climbing tree for the pastor's kids as they grew up. It was beautiful to look at during the fall, a pain to clean up after the fall, scary when covered in ice, and the symbol that winter had concluded each spring. Over the years, the parsonage had gone from pastor's home to Church office, to counseling center, to youth room, to eyesore. After the parsonage was removed, gravel was poured and a parking lot surrounded the giant old tree.

The tree had survived years of kids, storms, snow, as well as the trauma of buildings moving around it, heavy equipment pounding nearby, and huge trucks pouring gravel right up to the trunk. However, one season into the parking lot encircled tree, rumblings began to arise. The leaves made the gravel dangerously slippery through the fall. No one would park near it in winter or when storms were brewing for fear of finding a limb through their window after worship. The birds that called it home took target practice during the spring and summer on the cars below. Yes, the tree had survived every catastrophe known to man until it faced the greatest nemesis of all: A Church business meeting.

The only thing different about that unforgettable Wednesday night prayer service was the attendance. Crowds had come to

To Love and to Cherish from This Day Forward

pack the seats as if it were a University of Kentucky basketball game. But, it wasn't prayer that they came for... it was the town hall meeting to follow.

It seems that everyone had a memory of the great old tree and an opinion about her future. The deacons had come without a unified recommendation. The pastor wanted it gone. His wife did not. Faces turned red with anger and passion. Stories were told. Tears were shed. It was extremely entertaining to the youth who observed. Then, at a climactic moment, just before someone called for a vote, a to-this-point quiet influencer stood slowly to his feet, methodically reached into his coat pocket, taking out a piece of paper and his glasses. He dramatically secured the glasses to his face, unfolded the paper, and began to read:

Trees by Joyce Kilmer

I think that I shall never see a poem lovely as a tree.
A tree whose hungry mouth is pressed against the earth's
  flowing breast;
A tree that may in summer wear a nest of robins in her
  hair;
Upon whose bosom snow has lain; who intimately lives
  with rain;
Poems are made by fools like me, but only God can make
  a tree.

With that dramatic reading, he folded the paper, removed his glasses and quietly sat down. Silence was finally broken when someone called for the vote. By an extremely slim majority, the old tree lost. Early Thursday morning a crew that had already been contracted took the tree down before anyone could muster a broader opposition.

Twenty-five years of faithful service, biblical preaching, burying and marrying, saved the pastor from going down with that tree. A lesser pastor may not have been able to survive the Great Tree Controversy. But the ripples were felt for at least one whole season of memories.

Why was the question of taking down that tree so potentially destructive? It was not because the Church was filled with members of the Tree Huggers Society of America, local post 777. Nor was it because of the memories. It certainly wasn't because the Church didn't want to reach more people and provide places for them to park. The reason was simple, an age old problem with which virtually every conflicted Church struggles: Who is in charge here? How are decisions made? Is it the pastor or the whole staff that makes decisions? Are the deacons or elders calling the shots, or does the Church Council or Board have the most influence? Is it a Church Mother, or a quiet, significant giver that shifts the weight when judgments are finalized? Are the decisions driven by the needs or preferences of regular congregants, or are they made for the seeker, the not yet reached? How you answer these kinds of questions demonstrates the authority to which you bend as a Church... how you discern the Groom's best for His Son's Bride.

> *The beautiful, healthy Bride of Christ – His Church – discerns and submits to Him as her authority*

JESUS AND AUTHORITY

Jesus had much to say about the matter of authority. In Matthew 8 His travels took Him to Capernaum. A Roman officer met Him upon arrival. This officer came to Jesus, filled with compassionate concern for a special servant who was racked with pain. Although the officer never asked Jesus to come to his home, Jesus indicated that He would go there and heal his servant (a shocking claim, in and of itself). The genuine, gut level response of an obscure Roman officer has gone down in history.

> But the officer said, "Lord, I am not worthy to have you come into my home. Just say the word from where you are, and my servant will be healed. I know this because I am under the authority of my superior officers and I have authority over my soldiers. I only need to say, 'Go,' and they go, or 'Come,' and they come. And if I say to my slaves, 'Do this,' they do it." (Matt. 8:8-10 NLT)

Matthew described Jesus as stunned or amazed at the response of the officer. He was not stunned because what the officer said was farfetched. He was amazed at who it was who said it. Jesus immediately took advantage of this teachable moment. He turned to the crowd of Messiah seekers who were watching and listening and said, "I haven't seen *faith like this* in all the land of Israel" (Matt. 8:10 NLT, italics mine).

Did you see the link between demonstrated faith and submission to authority? The Roman officer may or may not have known much about faith, but he knew all about authority. While you may be curious about a command from a superior officer, you do not question that command. You obey it. You recognize that you are under authority. Understanding that Jesus had authority, in this case over disease and suffering, the officer simply asked Him to command the sickness to cease. Jesus' authority would not have been open to discussion or debate by the viral cells that gripped the servant's body. They would have had no choice but to submit to His authority.

Dr. Luke (and others) tells us of a day when Jesus and His first disciples determined to take a trip to the other side of the lake (Lk. 8:22f). There is something about the way the hills wrap around Lake Galilee, the way the winds sweep down from the mountains of the north and across the desert from the east, that cause it to be meteorologically volatile. Storms can and do come up pretty quickly. This particular day was just such an occasion. Without the benefit of Doppler radar, the guys set out on their cruise. Jesus, coming off of a busy season of teaching and healing, lay down and took a nap. While He was asleep the storm blew in. Luke uses phrases like *a fierce storm*, *threatened to swamp them*, and *they were in real danger*. In short, this was not an everyday squall.

The disciples were a weird mix of seasoned sailors and devoted landlubbers. My guess is that the landlubbers were the first to give in to the threatening waves. The sailors probably made a little fun of them. Then they began to recognize the jeopardy that loomed. Their first response was likely to grab hold of the others and begin to give orders. At some point the winds became so vigorous, the rain became so paralyzing, the lightening became so blinding, the thunder became so earsplitting, and the waves became so treacherous that everyone gave in to their circumstances, ran to Jesus and shouted, "Master, Master, we're going to drown" (Lk. 8:24 NLT)!

Between Matthew, Mark and Luke we learn that Jesus stood up (no easy trick on a small boat in such a storm), spoke to the wind and the waves, and issued a faith-*full*, command, saying, "Quiet! Settle down" (Mk. 4:39 MSG). The very next phrase from all three reports is: all was calm. Suddenly and inexplicably, this life-threatening situation was resolved because of His authority over nature. Seconds before, the fear of seasoned sailors sank into the same despair as those with less stable sea legs and resulted in a passionate cry for help. Now, all is calm. The winds, the rain, the lightening, the thunder and the waves all submitted to His instruction to quiet down. Even His disciples turned from panic to awestruck whispers, "Who is this man? ...When he gives a command, even the wind and waves obey him" (Lk. 8:25 NLT).

On yet another occasion we find Jesus arriving back in the Capernaum region, but now with growing, passionate opposition. After arriving at a home and teaching the crowd that gathered there, some people brought a paralyzed man to Jesus. Mark 2 fills in some of the gaps of this story of the faith of a few friends who brought their friend to Jesus to be healed. The very crowds that hung on His every word barred these devoted friends from getting their buddy to Jesus. So, filled with faith and creativity, the guys went to Plan B. They climbed to the roof, dug a hole and lowered the man through the opening, landing right in front of Jesus. Observing the faith exercised by these friends, Jesus forgave the paralyzed man of his sins. Religious leaders were enraged by Jesus' claim to forgive sins. They whispered among themselves, but Jesus heard the heart of their silence and responded to their objection. He said,

> "Is it easier to say to the paralyzed man 'Your sins are forgiven,' or 'Stand up, pick up your mat, and walk?' So I will prove that the Son of Man has the authority on earth to forgive sins." Then Jesus turned to the paralyzed man and said, "Stand up, pick up your mat, and go on home" (Mk. 2:9-11 NLT).

The issue at stake in this encounter was one of authority. Jesus had already demonstrated, again and again, that He had authority over all manners of disease. He had already revealed

His authority over the elements of nature. Now His authority over the clutches of sin is questioned. This is one of only a handful of times where Jesus set out to prove something to someone else. Having established His authority over disease, evil spirits and nature, He exercised that power as proof of His authority over sin. Did Jesus have such authority? Was the man truly forgiven of his sin? The answer was blazed into the memories of everyone present as a formerly paralyzed man leaped his way through the crowd and skipped his way down the street.

The questioning of Jesus' authority was a fairly frequent hobby of those whose pseudo authority was diminished by His authentic authority. In one incident, a variety of vested denominational types, credentialed seminary professors and miscellaneous preachers cornered Jesus. Mark writes that they "demanded, 'By what authority are you doing all these things? Who gave you the right to do them'" (Mk. 11:27-28 NLT)? It strikes me funny that in light of the issue of authority, they would demand something. This was a real clash of competing sources of authority. Rather than submitting to their demand, Jesus responded with a question (a habit of His), "Did John's authority to baptize come from heaven, or was it merely human?" Then He added, "Answer me" (Mk. 11:30 NLT)! While He did not submit to their demand, they immediately began to discuss an answer to His question (so, who really was in charge here?).

For political reasons, they determined that they could not answer Him. So He did not answer them. He immediately told them and those standing nearby a story (Mk. 12:1-12). The story was about a carefully prepared vineyard, the protective owner, some greedy and rebellious tenant farmers, faithful servants and the owner's much loved son. Everyone listening to the story got it. They all knew that God was the owner, the world was His vineyard, the prophets were His faithful servants, Jesus was His loved Son and those preachers, professors and leaders were the rebellious tenant farmers. They all knew that Jesus had answered their questions regarding the source of His authority. They also knew that He had jerked the rug out from under their self appointed authority (verse 12).

Jesus was not some power hungry despot. In fact, He seemed anxious to appropriate His remarkable authority to those who followed Him. When He called His first disciples we are told that He gave them authority for very specific purposes: to cast out evil spirits and to heal every kind of disease and illness (Matt. 10:1; Mk. 3:15). He authorized the former demoniac of the land of the Garasenes to "go back to your family, and tell them everything God has done for you" (Lk. 8:39 NLT). Following His resurrection, He authorized Mary to tell the disciples He was better than okay and they should meet Him at the designated spot. Before His ascension He gave them more authority. Through them, to His Church, He has given this same authority: make disciples.

Early in His ministry Jesus told a story about those who would one day stand before Him with a long list of noble accomplishments they had pursued according to His name (Matt. 7:21f). He ultimately called those people lawbreakers, evil doers, iniquity workers. Wow! Let's see... they called him (with their words) "LORD"... they prophesied, cast out demons, and did miracles... and they were evil doers? Really? It isn't so much what they did as how they did it. They did what they wanted to do rather than what He authorized them to do. They stepped outside of a right relationship (a proper relationship) with Him to pursue their own agenda. **The decision to decide rather than discern is something He takes very seriously.**

That said, the greatest lesson of authority from the life of Jesus is not found in His words or His actions. The greatest lesson is found in His example. Even though I've quoted this passage once before, we should pause and worship Him once more around these inspiring words:

> Though he was God, he did not think of equality with God as something to cling to. Instead, he gave up his divine privileges; he took the humble position of a slave and was born as a human being. When he appeared in human form, he humbled himself in obedience to God and died a criminal's death on a cross. (Phil. 2:5-8 NLT)

Every time His mission was challenged, whether by the enemy during temptation or by His best friend at a high and holy moment in Caesarea Philippi, or even internally during the quietness of His transparent Gethsemane prayers, He remained true to that mission. He set out with a clear vision of what the world would look like as a result of that mission and He saw it through to completion. He did not waver from the values that were those of His Father. He went to the very people He was sent to, no more and no less. He exercised a sensitive and keen sense of timing, made decisions strategically rather than randomly. **He submitted Himself to His Father's authority**.

THE FIRST CHURCH YIELDS TO HIS AUTHORITY

The first Church was largely made up of a group of people who had a history of trouble with submitting to authority. They rejected the authority of the cultural religious leaders of their day by choosing to follow Jesus. Like most of the residents of their part of the world, they resented the authority of the governing officials and their military counterparts.

Many of the key leaders of the early Church had personal histories filled with examples of their failure to submit to Jesus' authority. As He prepared to leave the Church, He carefully instructed them that obedience (submitting their will to His) was the one and only demonstration of true love. His personal representative, the Counselor, His own Spirit, would direct this yielding to His authority.

> *...they were not uniquely courageous people. But, they were a people deeply submitted to His authority for their community of faith.*

In Acts 1 and 2 we find the Jerusalem Church giving our first glimpse into what it was to yield to Jesus' instructions after His ascension. They were told to wait in Jerusalem until they were empowered. Then they were to begin the work of making disciples, starting where they were and spreading out from there. In hindsight, that looks like a great strategy. However, if I had been in that band of followers, I would have likely seen things differently. Jerusalem was the center of the down with Jesus movement of the day. Jerusalem was filled with religious leaders who arranged a most detestable set of circumstances that ultimately resulted in Jesus' crucifixion. Jerusalem was in the middle of a religious festival that meant emotional loyalty to the religion of the people was high. If I were there, I would have been tempted to think, "Let's start at the ends of the earth and work our way back here."

These early disciples chose to yield to Jesus' plan for their Church. The initial result was a one-day harvest of about 3000 souls. On the heels of that overwhelming response, community flourished, as it had not since Genesis 2. Miracles and proclaiming persisted all over the town. How did they have such courage? Acts 4 gives us a little insight. Peter and John were busy speaking to people about Jesus. The same adversaries Jesus had faced were very disturbed that Peter and John were continuing this mission (Acts 4:2). As the story unfolds, we discover that they were not uniquely courageous people. But they were a people deeply submitted to His authority for their community of faith. Because of that, they were able to obey His mission and, thus, demonstrate their love for Him.

Phillip was an early influencer in this new Church, being among the first deacons (servants) of the Church. He was submitted to Jesus' authority, fleeing Jerusalem during the persecution after Stephen's death, but not fleeing His mission. Phillip landed in Samaria and announced that the Messiah and God's Good Kingdom had come. The response was overwhelming. Crowds listened, demons scattered, the sick were healed, and "So there was great joy in that city" (Acts 8:8 NLT). At the height of this powerful response to Jesus, an angel came to Phillip and said, "Go south down the desert road that runs from Jerusalem to Gaza" (Acts 8:26 NLT).

Phillip had his mission field adjusted three times in just a few verses of Scripture. At first he was to target the already convinced widows in the Jerusalem Church. Next he was sent to the non-believing and new followers of Christ in Samaria. Finally he finds himself on a desolate desert road with no idea that he was about to be instrumental in sending God's Good News to a new continent. Why was Phillip usable? He simply discerned God's Voice and submitted to His authority.

Of course, all of the results of submitting to Jesus' authority were not as thrilling as the 3000 on Pentecost or the crowds in Samaria. Peter and John were imprisoned for their surrender to Jesus' authority. They and all of the followers of Jesus were threatened concerning their submission to His authority (Acts 4:17-18, 21). Stephen was stoned to death by an angry mob. James was killed with a sword, ordered by the government. And Paul?

> We patiently endure troubles and hardships and calamities of every kind. We have been beaten, been put in jail, faced angry mobs, worked to exhaustion, endured sleepless nights, and gone without food.... *We serve God whether people honor us or despise us*, whether they slander us or praise us.... We live close to death... Our hearts ache, We are poor... We own nothing...   (2 Cor. 6:4-10 NLT).

The first Church, the Bride of Christ, discerned and submitted themselves to the authority of Jesus. This is how they made decisions. They obeyed His mission and were able to see His vision of a redeemed world, starting in their world. They adopted and adapted His values. They went to H's assigned mission field. They followed His example.

Selah now represented Justus everywhere she went and to everyone with whom she spoke. His reputation was in some measure shaped by the way she lived. This was not something she took lightly. As the two became one, she was able to confidently finish a sentence for him with a smile and a wink. She picked up on his curiosities and passions. She saw people through his eyes. She gave up her own prejudices. She learned to honestly love those whom he loved. His authority in her life was expressed when she spent coins and how she spent time. As an act of trust toward him *and* respect for him, she used the betrothal as a time to discern how he decided, and submitted to *what* he decided. It was her goal to always please him in the decisions she made.

Healthy churches throughout the centuries have championed ways to do the same. Perhaps they did not use our contemporary catch phrases, but they did discern and submit to His authority... they did reap the rewards and paid the consequences of faithfulness in their time and place.

How might that look as we make decisions today? How does that process play itself out as we relate to one another (when we are with the family) and as we encounter those not yet touched by God's grace (when we are out and about)? Read on.

CHAPTER 10
HIS AUTHORITY, *ours*
(Discerning and Submitting in the 21st Century Church)

With a simple survey of Jesus' choice to hear from and submit to His Father's direction, as well as the example of the early Church following the lead of the Spirit, we are now ready to consider how submitting to His authority...how making decisions... how discerning and submitting to Him, is an expression of our new identity in Christ.

WHAT'S A PASTOR TO DO?

Just imagine... you are the pastor of a Church. It is late Wednesday night. You are sitting at your desk in your home. The midweek service is over. The Sunday morning subject has been planned for months. You have done some initial research, but the talk is just not coming together. In fact, you even wonder if the work that has been done to date represents a word from God or your own best plans. In the depths of your heart you know there will be people gathering on Sunday morning to hear a word from God, not you. You look at your calendar and see the week that lies ahead:

- There is a huge wedding on Saturday at 1:00, which means it will take up most of the morning and with a reception, keep you occupied into early evening.

- Saturday night has the note: *family date night* written by your spouse. You've spent precious little time with your family in recent weeks. The thought of canceling again is more than you can stomach.

- Friday night will be a long and tedious wedding rehearsal.

- The funeral of a faithful Church member is scheduled to begin at 10:00 Friday morning.

- You clearly have to spend some extra time with that family on Thursday.

Suddenly the phone rings and it is a fun friend from your past. He has a connection with a traveling music group, one of your personal favorites. He has called to give you the "really great news" that the group is coming through your town. They need a place to stay on Saturday night and, in return, would be thrilled to play a concert on Sunday morning.

Now imagine the weird mix of pressure and relief you suddenly feel. You don't have what you consider a clear word from God for the sermon Sunday, now just three days away. You don't have a day off before Sunday morning. You don't have a minute that's not already scheduled between now and then. You do have a friend and you do love an inspiring concert. You start to reason, "You know, our people would be so blessed by their music ministry; I know that I have in times past. Besides, they need a little bit of a break. After all, I was pretty hard on them this past Sunday." You poll your elders.

Simply put, how you decide what you decide reveals volumes about your discernment process... about the authority you bow to. A Christ-follower, a Christian family, or a Church that understands they serve under the authority of *Another* does not merely consider the *circumstances* when making decisions.

They do not, as in this case study, make the mission of the music group *their* mission. They don't make decisions for today based on what happened in the past.

> *How you decide what you decide reveals volumes about your sources of authority when you decide.*

They simply think only about what they are authorized to be/do – about the authority they serve under. What is His mission? (What has He said to us?) What is His vision? (What is He showing us?) What does He value? (Where must our treasure be?) Who is He touching around us? (How must we join Him in influencing them?)

The issue of Jesus' authority with His Bride – how we as followers of Christ and as churches make decisions – is a matter of discernment and submission. Churches as a community make decisions in a great variety of ways.

- Some make decisions based on past resourcing. They take last year's budget, which is just like the year before and the year before that, and they add or subtract dollars here and there without giving much thought to the current directives of the Groom.

- Some make decisions based on tradition. They look at last year's calendar and re-plan the same events simply because they are now *annual* for our Church.

- Others make decisions based on trends for tomorrow. They reason that the organ has got to be replaced with a small ensemble and the choir needs to disrobe in favor of a praise team. When asked, "Why?" by a small group within the Church who are genuinely curious, they answer, "Because it is the trend."

A Church (or a believer) that recognizes Jesus' authority in their midst may come to similar conclusions, but they do so in very different ways.

THE CHURCH CARTA

The *Magna Carta* was a document reluctantly agreed to by King John in 1215, (1) guaranteeing certain civil and political liberties to his people and in so doing, (2) relinquishing some of his own monarchical power. A *Carta* (or charter) has since come to describe a formal granting of specified rights by a sovereign.

Church is a people who have covenanted with each other. As a result of encountering Jesus, they have come to see that they actually were enslaved to the condition of sin; of disappointing Him repeatedly. In Him, they have been granted liberty. And when He sets you free, you are indeed free (John 8:31-36). However, they understand that liberty is not a license. Instead, it is an invitation to a new way of living that includes among other things, a desire to know our Sovereign's good will and submit to His authority. That desire finds both personal and community expressions as we make decisions.

One of the ways that churches express this aspiration in our day is through what I call a *Church Carta*... a charter statement that becomes a tool for the Church to use, as a congregation and as individuals, for *making* missional decisions. In recent years these *Carta* tools have come to include elements like a mission statement, a vision people can see and describe, value lists that are core to being the kind of people who live out such a mission and vision, and a defined mission field (or target audience) for playing out the mission.

Most churches (and most people) have ideas/tools like these and make decisions by them all the time. Sometimes the decisions impact how we get along with each other – among the Church. Sometimes they impact how we touch those still to meet our benevolent Groom – out and about. Sadly, they are too often unstated, unconscious and self-centered, based on human opinions rather than Divine discernment.

JESUS' AUTHORITY IN THE FAMILY…THE CHURCH

> *Our task is not to create a mission, but to discern what He has said. Then we are to articulate His mission in a way that the people who are our Church get it; head, heart, and hands.*

Regarding **mission**, the Bride of Christ… a Church… that sees themselves as under the authority of Jesus, wants to know what His mission is. They want to be consistent with that mission in every way. They realize that they are an army and He is the general. Therefore, His mission is non-negotiable. They accept that the mission of the Church is the mission of my Church and your Church. It is the mission of the church 2000, 200, and 20 years ago and will be the mission of the Church tomorrow. It is both a congregational *and* individual mission.

It is obviously important for a Church to take some time and look at the mission of Jesus throughout Scripture. They should start *there*, not with how others have sought to articulate the mission for their congregations. Once convinced and captured by that mission they should write it out in the language of the day and of their cultural setting. They (the people) should cling to the mission, implement it, and build memories by living it daily – not a corporate mission, but a community mission.

While the value of the exercise of discovering God's mission can be incredible for a congregation, it is vital that we guard against coming up with a mission statement that suits us. We do not have that right or authority. The mission is His and, as I argued in chapters 1-4, it is already clearly articulated. Our task is not to create a new, cool statement, but to discern what He has said about what He is doing then convey His mission in a way that the people who are our Church get it; head, heart, and hands.

Vision is different from mission. Vision is also discerned, but not as words. Vision is a picture, a dream, given by Christ to His Bride so we can recognize when His mission is being achieved. Vision is often foggy at first, but becomes clearer as we get closer, and always parallels His mission.

Vision can be informed by a number of factors. For example, God has provided gifts for His Church so His vision can become reality. So it is important that His people gain a grasp of how they are gifted (remember, gifts are to the Church, not to the individual). His vision is usually unusual, and almost always bigger than our best guess, so it is also crucial that we have an awareness of the lives of the people that our people rub elbows with, those who are currently outside of His Kingdom. It seems to me that vision is also influenced by the gifts and journeys of those who are the spiritual leaders of the Church at this time.

While mission is unchanging, vision is a picture from God to *this* Church at *this* place at *this* time. God's vision for the Church where you are now is not likely the same as the vision that He cast to that same congregation twenty years ago, or the one that will gather together twenty years from now. As the faith community changes, their gift-mix changes as well. As the mission field transitions, the needs around the Church family fluctuate. Since you are dealing with a community, a living organism, rather than an organization, God's vision will always be more fluid than fixed.

This fluidity might look like a slight tweak or a total overhaul. A vision comes from God as surely as the mission did. The mission however has been preserved for us in inspired Scripture. God's vision emerges as a result of a deepening relationship with Him. As He speaks to His Church by His Spirit through ways like His Word, prayer, circumstances, and through one another, that relationship is strengthened and our vision of what He is doing in, through and around us grows clearer. As He encounters and encourages us, we submit to His authority in our lives, personally and communally.

I once served a Church that told me that they valued people who did not yet know Jesus. Nonetheless, every time we discussed matters relating to those people, the subject was changed. There was, however, a constant passion. Thirty years earlier, under the leadership of a fine pastoral team and the Holy Spirit, they established a daycare. It was the first Christian daycare in that part of their state. It was established in order to meet the needs of a new, suburban community and meet new people, some of whom were without Christ.

Over the years, policies and personnel had developed in such a way that the organization now existed largely to perpetuate itself. Needs in the neighborhood had changed as the residents had aged. Government funded programs and a growing number of private corporation daycares had increased competition. But if someone suggested that the Church move out of the daycare business, a sound was heard like a mighty rushing wind! While the *stated* value was pre-Christian people, the *real* value was daycare. Values are very powerful influencers when decisions are made.

Mission does not change; vision changes as the Body of Christ changes; and **core values** mature as the Body of Christ grows toward the image of Christ. That is true in the life of the person on spiritual journey in whom you are investing, it is true in the small group to which you belong, and it is true in the local community of believers of which you are a part. Truly core values are actually pretty easy to identify.

> *Every Church must ask: Are the things we value the things God values?*

I remember my first experience of being ordered to evacuate the City of New Orleans due to an approaching hurricane. The notice came suddenly and we had to make decisions about what we really valued. What we packed as irreplaceable were things like family photos, computer discs, tax files, etc. When push comes to shove, the things you grab that are considered irreplaceable represent a kind of core value. Every Church has them. Every believer has them. Ultimately we must all ask: Are the things we value the things God values?

Our disciple making process must move past a fixation on facts or an addiction for certain behaviors. We must create an environment that nourishes and nurtures His values. We must discover, challenge, apply and internalize those values. Only when the Bride of Christ owns the values of our Groom, do we naturally make decisions as those who are under His authority.

One of my favorite questions when consulting with pastors is, "So, who is your competition around here?" Over the last few years I have asked that question hundreds of times. Easily better than 90% of the responses have had to do with another Church in their denomination, or another evangelical congregation in the community. On very rare occasions have pastors instinctively identified the competition of the world, the flesh or the devil.

> *We want to choose who we do Church for. In reality, we must discern who God has designed us to be Church for.*

Although untested, my hypothesis is that the people of God who make up a local Church, asked the same question, would respond similarly. While the response does reveal something about core values, it also reveals a great deal about the sense that you have about your **mission field**… who you believe your target audience to be. If your competition is thought to be another Church of believers, then you likely target "church people" when making decisions about what and how to do things. The question of mission field impacts everything you do – when and where you gather, if or how you build buildings, how you spend money, how you search for pastoral staff, and so on. It is essential that a Church seek the face and heart of God in order to understand whom He has placed on their radar. Selfishness is a huge temptation here. We want to choose who we do Church for. In reality, we must discern whom God has designed us to *be* Church for.

JESUS' AUTHORITY WHILE WE ARE OUT AND ABOUT

These same basic aspects of decision making (of discerning and submitting to Jesus' authority) have a direct relationship to how a believer or a Church impacts those around us who do not know Christ as we are out and about. A Church submits to Jesus' authority concerning **mission** when they adopt His mission, not as *a part of* their mission, but *as* their mission. In the last two decades of the twentieth century, many leaders called the Church back to a sense of real mission. In the 1st decades of the twenty-first century the word missional has been popularly used to describe this passion. Whether the word used was purpose, mission or dream, the idea was similar: be driven by a cause greater than your own – outside of your own. Recognize His mission and at any and all costs, make it yours.

Jesus calls the Church (the Bride) the key keeper for the Kingdom of God (Matt. 16). Christ has given the Church His authority to unlock the doors of His Kingdom so others can enter. The Church in this text is pictured as marching against the gates of hell. The metaphor Jesus chose was *gates*. Gates are not offensive weapons. Armies do not charge fortresses carrying gates. Gates are defensive weapons. Gates are what armies charge. The imagery is unmistakable. **Jesus expected His Church to be on His mission.** To the *on mission* Church He promised the gates of hell would not be able to deter their attack.

In the Great Commission passages the Church is described as under the authority of the Commander in Chief, on mission... going, making disciples, baptizing, teaching to obey, and sent announcing the Good News that there is forgiveness of sins for all who will turn to Jesus.

In John 20 and Acts 1 the Church is described as Holy Spirit empowered, sent in the same way as Jesus was sent, on the same mission, starting where they are right now and stretching out toward the whole world.

At Pentecost the Church – believers out and about – went person to person announcing God's Good News boldly (not rudely) and in such a way that a diverse culture could understand what they were saying.

The Church exists to be on one Mission: His! His mission was to the world. Jesus never lost this focus. His first Church did not lose it. This mission is shared by all churches of all times in all places and all cultures. The mission is non-negotiable. Healthy churches choose to lay aside their own interests (literally to submit) in order to address missional issues, evaluating every decision by the degree to which they, as a people, are being disciples of Jesus who are making disciples of Jesus.

> *Vision is a portrait of what your part of the world looks like because God's people are on God's mission, here and now!*

A Church today submits to Jesus' authority concerning **vision** when they begin to see what their part of the world would look like if it were filled with redeemed people. Jesus approached His service with a clear vision from the Father. He knew what a person who loved God with all of his heart, soul, mind and strength would look like. He could see people who were far from God, washing the feet of others, giving cold water under His authority and announcing the great news that God's Kingdom had come in word and deed. This vision was so *clear* to Him that He could instill it in others by telling stories and practicing actions. If you or I do not have such a vision...do not pursue such a dream...then the people we affect will ramble about anywhere (Prov. 29:18), tying their faith to programs, buildings, traditions and even an old oak tree.

True vision is a picture that God paints for our lives – for how we live. It is a picture of how His mission looks, accomplished in this part of His world and through this group of His people.

A vision like that can never be created by consensus.
Consensus generally means everyone gets a little slice of the pie. Consensus built vision statements often reflect opinions, not discerned words from God: no one gets exactly what s/he wanted so, somehow, everyone wins... except God. No, vision is not created *by* consensus. However, vision does create consensus.

As of this writing, the United States continues in what it calls a war on terrorism. Whenever a people recognize themselves to be at war, things change. Shortly after the attacks of September 11, 2001, the members of Congress gathered on the steps of the Capitol as a show of solidarity for the American people. In that setting and completely unplanned, this diverse group of people began to sing "God Bless America." The event was carried on television across the country and around the world. Someone had to have been first to sing. I don't know who that was. But when they started, everyone else joined in spontaneously. The moment was moving. Someone's vision created consensus among a people.

Now, years later, Congress is again on Capitol Hill. They are working on whatever the fix of the week is for the country. Vision has been blurred by time and an inward focus on personal political doctrines. The debate rages over versions of bills that are right for the country. Chief leaders are meeting daily, chiseling out pieces of legislature to please all of the interested parties. When these laws go to the President to sign, it will be a consensus. No one gets what s/he wants, so everyone somehow wins. I suppose that's the way law writing works. But it is not visionary...it does not inspire the heart to see anew.

> *Vision from God will be all about Him and them, not all about us.*

A vision for life while we are out and about is not something that a Church works up. Vision is something that God sends out. Inasmuch, God's vision will have God's focus on those people not yet reached with His Good News. Vision from God will be all about Him and them, not all about us. It will be far reaching, bigger than life itself, inspiring. Vision will be an increasingly clear picture of what our corner of the world will look like when His Church is on His mission here. Once discerned, vision becomes reality when people submit to it.

A Church submits to Jesus' authority concerning **values** when they begin to own His values, whether gathered or scattered. Values are how we make the day to day, nuts and bolts decisions. An authentic Church must grow to value the same things that Jesus values so their decisions will naturally be more Christ like.

One of His chief (or core) values was people. He valued all people. While He certainly valued those who were His followers, He did not do so at the expense of the people that were not yet touched by His message. He went to Roman government employees (like tax collectors) and officials, to the diseased (unclean), to sinners (immoral, unethical, and insane). He also went to the religious who were genuinely seeking to know God

(Andrew, Nicodemus). Once when He was ridiculed for this value, Jesus responded, "Healthy people don't need a doctor – sick people do" (Matt. 9:12 NLT). Zacchaeus, his family and much of Jericho were stunned that Jesus took such interest in him. To their amazed stares Jesus explained, "For the Son of Man came to seek and save those who are lost" (Lk. 19:10 NLT). He valued these people so much that He gave His life for them. He valued them so much that He sent His followers to continue to love and announce Good News to them.

Many of today's churches have seen the importance of identifying values. As a result they have formed lists of values that they diligently teach to new or aspiring congregants. Unfortunately the process many churches have used is more like that of the business world than the Kingdom. Resulting behaviors have been limited to the institutional setting. For example, most Church value lists include a statement like, 'we value unchurched, pre-Christian or lost people'. As a demonstration of that particular value, the Church (institutionally) will have a Welcome Center, greeters, user friendly language, contemporary use of technology, harvest events and so on.

None of these are inherently bad. But all of them are corporate responses to a value. It is something like a corporation saying they value potential clients so they keep their offices in order, they hire friendly voices to answer phone calls, they provide filled coffee pots in waiting rooms. The problem is that in the corporate world it is okay to value a potential client during working hours but when you are off the clock to live as though that person does not exist. In the Church this kind of thinking is unacceptable. In fact it does more harm than good.

The people of God must own His values. They must be internalized. Only then will behavior *naturally* reflect God's work in us. Only then will it be the *normal* activity of our day to see the unchurched around us, while we are out and about, as He sees them and to respond as ambassadors of His mission.

A Church submits to Jesus' authority regarding a **mission field** (or target audience) when they go to whom He has sent them. Jesus consistently conducted a targeted approach during His earthly ministry. It stands to reason that He would be unswerving with that action today. He went to people who were not healthy, to those who were spiritually sick. When He first appointed His disciples He sent them to the people of Israel. Specifically, He told them not to go to the Gentiles or Samaritans (Matt. 10:5-6). Later He expanded their mission field. The woman at the Samaritan well went into Sychar to announce Jesus. The demoniac went to the ten towns of the eastern shore of the lake.

When Jesus told the story of the farmer scattering seed (Lk. 8:4-15; Matt. 13:1-23; Mk. 4:1-20), He used a great pronoun. Jesus did not say that the farmer scattered seed around *the* field or in *a* field. He said the farmer scattered seed around *his* field. That is, around a field that he owned. This was not a random scattering of seed. It was a purposeful scattering of seed in an assigned field. The reality that some seed fell on paths or in the gravel or in a thorn patch did not change the fact that there was a target for the scattering.

The disciples went to Jerusalem (Acts 1 and 2), Philip went to Samaria (Acts 8), and Paul and Barnabas were set apart by the Holy Spirit and the Antioch Church for a special assignment (Acts 13). Timothy was assigned to Ephesus (1Tim. 1:3). It has always been consistent with the character and mission of Jesus to have a mission field in mind.

In fact, every Church targets someone. I grew up in a small, rural Church that targeted people who did not work on Sunday morning, who owned a tie (and would wear it), and who appreciated gospel music with a honky-tonk beat. We did not profile our target, but we did make decisions based on those people being present and comfortable and engaged.

Not too far from our home now is a county gun club. Those who belong to this club do not carry their guns into a field and start shooting in any and all directions. Instead, the field is sprinkled with hay bales that have targets marked on them. The club members do not aim in the general direction of the bales, specifically at the bales, or even at the targets. They meticulously aim at the center of the targets.

Dan Southerland has noted that targets all have centers

> *The question is not, "Are you deciding for someone?" The question is, "Are you deciding for Jesus?"*

(*Transitioning: Leading Your Church Through Change*, 49f); that is what you aim for – the center. In conferences Dan explains that targets also have outer rings – those are also completely acceptable places to leave a mark. They are not what you aim for, but they are what you sometimes hit. Every Church is targeting someone. If it is not stated that way, it is demonstrated in a thousand ways. The question is not, "Are you deciding for someone?" The question is, "Are you deciding for Jesus?"

Mission fields do *not* exclude anyone; they only provide a context for discerning and submitting. What makes a mission field good and godly is the way that a Church goes about identifying it. Any process that is not bathed in prayer (discerning and submitting, not choosing) and is not consistent with the audiences to which Jesus went (those who need a doctor, those who are wandering as though lost) is not likely to result in submission to our Groom along His mission. It's us doing Church for our sake.

The Church, as a believer and as a people, watches the LORD and follows His example. **We are not a cabinet set up to offer advice to Jesus. He is the Sovereign and we are His Bride.** He is the One with authority – the One in charge. We discern His mission, see His vision, own His values and love the people who make up our mission field.

Churches and believers who master Christ-honoring decision-making grow to see the Groom as the One who is on mission and themselves as His helpmeet, living only and always under His authority.

CHAPTER 11
our DELIGHT, HIM
(Worshipping and Adoring Him)

OH WHAT A NIGHT!

We were four college students attending small schools in Kentucky and Tennessee. Friends since junior high, none of our individual families had money to finance a trip home to Atlanta, Georgia. If we had the ability to build a new car from the best parts of all of our old cars, it might have been safe enough for the journey. So when a trip back to Georgia was in order, we chose the most promising vehicle of the week, pooled our limited and always dwindling funds, and packed leftovers for snacks. Of course the rewards far outweighed the sacrifice – time with family, clean clothes, bags of groceries, and a little gift-cash for the trip back.

It was November of 1978. We had been home for Thanksgiving and were making our way back to Appalachia. Being the fearless foursome, we opted to bypass the more direct interstate route and journey as our forefather's would have, directly through the mountains – on paved roads of course. Specifically, we crossed the Great Smoky Mountains between Cherokee, North Carolina and Gatlinburg, Tennessee. If you've ever traversed the mountains at that point you know that the road is steep (for an old, overloaded car) and the roads are crooked (so crooked that you could drain your battery blowing your horn at your own brake lights). Add to this the poorly designed plan of driving across the mountains late at night and you have all the makings of a next day newspaper headline: *Bad Car + Dumb-stupid College Students = Mountainside Tumble!*

God was good to us that night. There was no smoke on the mountains. Although it took twice as long as it should have, we finally crested the incline and started down. Right at that apex is a Scenic Overlook. It was so dark in the valley below that there was no way we could look over anything and we were a carload of city kids predisposed to overwhelming fear at the slightest animal noise, but we stopped anyway.

The night was still. No wind, no fog. With nothing to see in the valley, we looked up. Thank God, we looked up. The sky was the darkest dark that had ever been. It was the kind of dark that was actually rich with color. The shimmering cloth, stretched from horizon to horizon, was pierced with pinholes. Each hole let those of us on this side of the sky look through to the other side. The brightness of the stars was hypnotizing. We stood in a circle, staring, unable to speak. The only interruption from the captivating show was the steam rising from our gaping mouths into the cold, November air. Spontaneously we grasped each other's hands. Without a word of instruction we broke out in familiar songs of praise. Without assignment, we prayed. Tears flowed with no provocation. I don't know how long we stood there. I'm not sure how we concluded it was time to go. It all happened so naturally – so supernaturally. We stopped. God was there. We saw Him. **Worship was all we could do.**

The Church has been a worshiping community since its inception. Unless the people of God worship, are they even really a Church? In recent years the topic of worship has become the cue ball on the pool table of the Church – constantly knocked around; bouncing from one bank to the other; crashing mercilessly into other issues; and tumbling way too often into pockets it was not designed for. Many people who are reading these words have left a Church or battled within a Church over this very issue. Some have even used the phrase worship wars to describe this struggle. This is so unfortunate. Wars always have enemies. So when a Church engages in a worship war, who is the enemy? Is it a member of the pastoral staff? Is it another believer who merely has different tastes? How delighted the true enemy of the Church must be when he can turn us against one another with the very thing that the Father desires, the worship of His people. How did worship become such an unnatural subject for a people who were made for worship?

I will never forget that night on the mountain in east Tennessee. In community, undistracted, without discussion, we saw God. **Worship erupted.** We could not stop it. We would not if we could have. That was my first glimpse of what I think Christ longs for from His Bride. When we light up at His presence, we reveal Him to others. We are drawn close to His side. Our lives, families, and communities are changed. When we see Him, we worship... it is all we can possibly do.

WHAT IS WORSHIP?

A subject of such focus has not gone without attention from movers and shakers of the Church of recent decades. Indeed, some of our greatest thinkers and most admired practitioners have weighed in with excellent definitions of worship. Some confined their thoughts to the Church gathered for worship events. Others use a much broader net for the subject of worship. My thinking has been inspired and informed by many more than I can name. Since it has been my purpose from the outset of this book to learn from the redemptive story captured in the pages of Scripture, let's do that here as well, by looking at some of the words that unpack worship in the Bible.

WORSHIP WORDS

Many words are used throughout the Bible to communicate the idea of worship. Each represents an inspired point along the spiritual journey of those people supernaturally used by God to pen the Bible. A survey of some of those words has helped me to begin to see the comprehensiveness of all that is involved in the wonder of worship. In the Hebrew Old Testament, the most prominent words used were:

- *Shachah* = to bow down or to prostrate oneself
- *Hodah* = to give thanks
- *Yada* = to know (relationally) God
- *kesed* = covenant love
- *saghidh* = to fall down
- *avad* = to serve
- *yare* = to fear the LORD
- *ragaz* = to tremble
- *darash* = to eagerly seek the LORD
- *qara* = to call on the Name of the LORD

As this survey reveals, worship involved action for the people of God. Worship included physical actions such as bowing, falling, serving, trembling and seeking. Worship also included actions of the heart like giving thanks, fearing and calling (a kind of trusting). Worship included relational actions like a knowing intimacy and covenanting together. Worship was not something to be observed, it was something you participated in with every fiber of your being. Worship meant reverence of mind and body; it meant adoration, obedience and service. **Worship was more than an event; it was a way of life that spilled over into the community of faith.**

In the Greek New Testament the concepts introduced through the ages continued to describe worship. However, a couple of ideas were added to the mix. These words enlarged a view of worship for those who were experiencing a more intimate relationship with God through His Son, Jesus.

- *latreuo* = rendering honor or paying homage
- *proskuneo* = to kiss toward, to kiss the hand, or to bow down. Signifies humble adoration.

Insight into worship was expanded in the New Testament to include these more relational ideas. Having introduced God as more than Father; rather as the close, present Abba (daddy), Jesus ushered in the potential for a more intimate handle on worship. Followers of Jesus could render honor as they would to a respected parent. They could pay homage as they would to a sovereign. They could kiss as they would a close kin. Yet, they bowed down as they would only to the Creator. Still, worship was to be much more than an event. In addition to all that worship was for the people of God before Jesus, worship became warmly adoring our loving, spiritual daddy, through His Son and our big brother, Jesus.

Translators have struggled through the centuries to capture all that is wrapped up in worship in a word or two. As English translators began their wrestling match with the language, there were two words that most frequently appeared:

- *weorthscipe* = the concept of worthiness
- *worthship* = to attribute worth to an object or a person

These words share obviously similar notions. God is worthy. Whether or not anyone, anywhere, at any time ever recognized that, it would not change His worthiness. To attribute worth to God represents a freewill decision to worship Him with life. It is not merely a decision to get out of bed on Sunday morning and head to the Church building. Worship is a lifestyle choice: it is to recognize that God alone is worthy. This is not something we do just when we gather in a cathedral. It must be a way we live in the ordinary days of life.

> *When I see God, when I hear God, when I agree with God – that He is worthy—I worship God!*

Worship is in this respect a kind of confession, agreeing with God about a Truth that He has established. He is worthy; of this there is no doubt. When I see Him and hear Him and agree with Him about His worthiness, I am worshiping Him. This agreeing is so much more than an intellectual ascent. This is an agreement touching every aspect of my being. This is an affirming of His supreme value.

In spite of all this academic sounding review, worship is really very simple. Although it might include events, it is decidedly not an event. It is a life attitude that attributes to God His worth – stating and affirming, in word and deed, His supreme value. It is an attitude that involves the soul, body, mind and strength of the worshiper in actions of obedience, adoration and service. It is honoring God as Supreme. Worship is…

- recognizing God's presence now, and celebrating Him here

- stopping, acknowledging and seeing God in this very moment

- supernaturally natural for those who know Him, by experience, through Jesus

WHO IS WORSHIP FOR ANYWAY?

> *Worship is not for us, about us, focused on us or related to our preferences. It is related to God's worth.*

I suspect that if a Church could ever embrace an answer to this question, 99% of the quarrelling related to worship would cease. In short, worship is not for us, it is for God. Worship is not about us. It is about God. Worship is not focused on us. It is focused on God. Worship is not related to our preferences. It is related to God's worth. Worship is not a matter of event style. Worship is a matter of life substance.

Football is not my favorite sport. In fact it is way down the list – too many committee meetings! However, very many people do love the game. College football stadiums across the country will attract crowds that swell to over 100,000 rabid fans. These fans usually go to the parking lot hours early to cook feasts that rival a holiday meal in size and scope. They all dress in the same color clothing in order to mess up the HD televisions of millions of people who choose to watch the contest at home. The fans provide a distinct benefit for teams. It is called the home field advantage. Sometimes they are even referred to as the twelfth player.

Basically a football game has four *people* components: you have the fans who are virtual participants in the game; the players who actually play the game; the coaches who watch and direct the game; and the referees who watch and judge the game. It has occurred to me that in a way many of our worship gatherings have taken on something of a football flare.

We gather in stadiums regardless of size (called worship centers, auditoriums or sanctuaries) wearing the acceptable uniform of the day. Often we come early to talk with one another about whether our Church team will win or lose today.

The congregants play the role of the fans in the stand. We are for our team, but we are not playing the game. Instead, we sit in the stands (pews) and watch. We cheer when they do well and we grieve when they do not. The choir, praise team/band, worship pastor and teaching pastor are seen as the players. God is viewed as the coach, providing strategic, behind the scenes direction to the event. The personnel committee, elders or deacons are the referees, more formally judging the event. They allow the event to continue until some penalty occurs. Then they bring the penalty to the attention of the players, the coach and the fans. Sometimes they even throw players or a coach out of the game.

While an entertaining notion, these assignments are far removed from where they should be. A more accurate use of the football metaphor would be to see the players as the congregants, at least those who are faith convinced believers and followers of Jesus. They are the people who worship. The coaches (who should likely see themselves as player/coaches) might better be seen as those worship prompters: the choir, praise team/band, worship and teaching pastors. Their role is to prompt the people of God to worship *as* they themselves worship. The stands are filled with an audience of One: God. He is the object of our worship. He is the reason we engage in worship as a lifestyle and join with others in worship at an event. The referee? Perhaps the Spirit of God; He is the One who presents our worship in an acceptable way to the Father. He is the One who is grieved when we say we are worshiping but fail to truly worship.

In His famous conversation with a lady by the well in Samaria (John 4), Jesus taught that the time has now come when worship like this is not tied to a physical location or a cultural heritage. Rather, it is in direct relationship to the spirit and the truth. The first believers worshiped together each day as they served the Kingdom in and around the temple and from house to house (Acts 2). Cornelius and his whole household broke out in spontaneous worship in their home upon hearing and receiving the Good News of a Savior (Acts 10). Paul and Silas worshiped in prison (Acts 16). The place or the tradition was not the issue.

In a great variety of places and times the people of God have the potential of encountering the LORD of the universe and breaking out in true worship. Worship is all about Him. Worship is all for Him. We are the beneficiaries of true worship, not the focus. In worship, when we acknowledge and embrace His presence, we are forever transformed at our very core.

JESUS ON WORSHIP

Jesus' earthly life was decorated with worship from the very beginning. Each year as we peek into the stall behind the Bethlehem Inn, we see a blue collar carpenter, his young wife, poor shepherds, wealthy kings, the inhabitants of heaven, animals of the field, stars in the sky and nature itse f – **everyone and everything worshiping the newborn King!** During His childhood we are told that He grew in favor with God and all who knew Him. His parents were both pictured as devout in their faith. We can only presume their devotion included typical family worship habits common to their faith (for example, see Deut. 6:1-9). By the time Jesus was twelve He was participating with His parents in what may have been an annual pilgrimage to Jerusalem for worship. When Jesus went public with His ministry, He did so with a group of people who were gathered in worship of God along the side of the Jordan River (Lk. 3:21f, Mk. 1:9f, Matt. 3:13f, Jn. 1:29f).

Jesus' ministry was sprinkled with times of worship. Sometimes He worshiped alone. Often He worshiped with His disciples. Occasionally He worshiped with larger crowds. He frequented synagogues. He was regularly in Jerusalem. He prayed, He sang, He read Scripture, He taught, He celebrated and He grieved when people rejected God's Kingdom. He stopped in everyday life to see and acknowledge the Father. Worship was not something He did – it was the essence of who He was –

> *Worship was not something Jesus did; it was the essence of who Jesus was.*

intimately related to the Father, bowing to Him, kissing His hand, embracing Him, submitting to Him.

Jesus taught about worship on several occasions. He told that dear woman in Samaria that worship was not about a geographical place; it was about a Divine face. He said, "...the time is coming – indeed it's here now – when true worshipers will worship the Father in spirit and in truth. The Father is looking for those who will worship him that way. For God is Spirit, so those who worship him must worship in spirit and in truth" (Jn. 4:23-24 NLT). He told the enemy of the Church that we are created to "worship the LORD your God and serve only him" (Matt. 4:10 NLT). He accused religious leaders of making worship a farce (Mk. 7:7).

After all was said and done, Jesus met His disciples on a hill outside of Galilee. In that setting He delivered what has come to be called the Great Commission. Prior to Matthew's account of those orders are some observations that God is using to teach me much about worship.

> Then the eleven disciples left for Galilee, going to the mountain where Jesus had told them to go. When they saw him, they worshiped him – but some of them doubted. (Matt. 28:16-17 NLT)

It strikes me that worship was in this case (and maybe in any case), precipitated by a willingness to get where Jesus has instructed you to go. For those disciples it meant physically leaving Jerusalem or wherever they may have scattered after the crucifixion and gathering at a specific mountain in Galilee. For me that often means something different. I know that Jesus is grieved when I choose to sin, to opt for something that is less than His best for me. I am certain He is disappointed when I miss time with Him because I am too busy or when I spend the time at a particular place (a personal prayer closet, in small group, or in the worship center) but my mind is a million miles away. Getting where He has told me to go means addressing those kinds of things. It is not enough to go where I want to go. I must go where He has indicated He expects me to go, not necessarily physically, but in spirit and in truth.

Those first disciples had to go where He told them to go in order to see Him and so must I.

- I simply cannot see Him when I am facing another direction

- I cannot see Him when I am distracted by other things around me

- I cannot see Him when I am so busy that the next deadline blinds me

The disciples did not worship until they saw Him. They might have prayed. They could have sung. They may have updated each other with announcements. But there was no worship until they saw Him. And I cannot worship until I see Him.

Worship was for those disciples the natural reaction to seeing Him. They saw Him because they were where He expected them to be. But (and I find such delight in this observation) some of them still wrestled with doubt. Doubt? You have GOT to be kidding! They saw three and a half years of miracles. They witnessed His death and had heard that He was raised from the dead. They were convinced enough that the rumor might be true that they gathered in Galilee on a specific mountainside. Now they were standing face to face with the resurrected LORD. They went, they saw, they broke out in worship – but they still did not have Him and His Kingdom figured out – they still doubted.

True worship – the kind that is supernaturally natural for those who follow Jesus – is precipitated by the worshiper getting where the LORD is. Once there, we can see Him. When we see Him, worship is all we can do. We don't have to be timid about our doubts because they do not surprise Him. He is not bothered that I can't figure it all out. I can love Him with all my mind without understanding Him completely. I can worship Him without comprehending fully all that He is.

WORSHIP AND WORSHIP EVENTS ARE NOT THE SAME THING!

Unfortunately in our day worship has been reduced to worship events in many churches. An event does not have to depend on the Spirit of God or the Truth (Jesus) to occur. In fact many scheduled, timed, planned services are evaluated in ways other than those Jesus suggested for spiritual, truth-based worship. Worship events are

> **Worship events are often more concerned with getting Jesus to join us where we have gathered than with getting to the place where Jesus is.**

often more concerned with getting Jesus to join us where we have gathered than with getting to the place where Jesus is. Worship events are sometimes less concerned with seeing Him than with being seen by Him (or by others). Worship events are at times so cognitive that we seem more concerned with figuring God out than celebrating His presence. Worship events are at times more emotional catharsis than loving adoration. All of these factors have created an environment in which worship can be described as a war. By these descriptors worship is not the natural function of the Bride of Christ. Rather, it is the unnatural, competitive activity of a religious organization.

Most worship events include all of the right elements. The ingredients do not seem to be the problem. Rather than wrestling with the less concrete issues of the work of God's Spirit in and through those elements, churches tend simply to focus on the elements. Our evaluations are often filled with the wrong questions: Did the prayer offend anyone? Was the timing from hymn to prayer to hymn efficient? Was there any dead time in the program? What about the length of the sermon? Was it too long? Was it too short? Was it just right? Was there a seamless theme from beginning to end of the event? How about the response? Did people move forward or fill out a card or stay for a dialog session? I am not suggesting that the Church, the Bride of Christ, should not constantly monitor the development of their worship events. The problem may not be in what we ask. It may be in what we fail to ask, or fear to ask. We do not ask about God's presence. We do not ask whether people stopped assessing the leaders and started addressing the King.

> **When we see Him, worship is all we can do!**

It is completely possible to have a year's worth of high quality worship events and never worship. It is equally possible for people to encounter God in worship where no service has been planned. A small group in a home might encounter God and be stilled by the awareness of His presence. A family listening to music in the car as they vacation might sudden upon the realization that God is there. One person might sit alone at his kitchen table reading the Bible when the moments of discipline are converted to moments of delight as God lights up the pages of a passage. A group of college students might recognize God in the heavens along a lonely road.
Recognizing God in times like these should be the natural result

of familiarity with Him developed in the practice of gathering for worship with the Church. When we recognize Him, we stop and worship breaks out!

The goal of worship as a simple indication of what it is to be Church is not to improve the flow or to change the style of worship events. The goal is worship. Not just to worship when we gather, but to see Jesus (our Groom) at work around us all the time... as a matter of lifestyle... and when we see Him, to adore Him in that very moment. Living like that lends integrity and authenticity to our worship when we gather.

We must simply and courageously evaluate worship in terms of the recognition of God's presence and the change that inevitably follows an encounter with Him. In a sense, worshiping the One True God in spirit and in truth separates us from others. It is not enough to do many good things, improving our communities, our families, and the qualities of our own lives. Unless we worship God, we are not Church.

God's top ten list includes the command for us to worship God. True worship is therefore an act of obedience. This has many implications. Perhaps the most important is this: **to meet together with the announced purpose of worship, and then do anything less is an act of disobedience.**

God has provided His Spirit to facilitate our worship and the Truth to guide our worship. To worship is to glorify Him – Father, Son and Holy Spirit. It is to ascribe honor to Him, to acknowledge Him – His attributes. His acts and His very being. It is to reveal God in this world and to our world. When our worship reveals more of us than it does of Him, we have failed to glorify God and therefore, failed to worship...failed to adore the One we love.

Adoration is about the only word the neighbors could use to describe Selah when it came to Justus. From day one – with the mud flying all around the shop and Justus trying to look cool about it, she just adored him. Everyone noticed it. When they were together she was in awe of every word he spoke. When they were apart he was the subject of every sentence. She blushed with emotion every time he noticed her... and he noticed her all the time. It was the kind of true love that even a stranger recognized when they walked down the street. It was what every bride and every groom longed for. It is what The Groom longs for with His Bride as well.

CHAPTER 12
our DELIGHT, HIM
(Gathered *and* Scattered)

Okay. We have explored the big picture – skimming a rock across the surface of the subject of worship. How is our identity as the Bride of Christ expressed by a life of adoration? How does worship demonstrate that we are embracing this new identity? How is worship expressed when we are with the family (gathered) and when we are out and about (scattered)?

WORSHIP WHEN WE ARE WITH THE FAMILY

The Church...and a Church...is made up of people who are faith convinced that Jesus is who He says He is. By worship when we are with the family I simply mean worship as a way of being when we are with our Church... when we are

> *Believers in Jesus should never find themselves as observers when it comes to worship.*

gathered. There are at least two critical issues regarding worship from the post conversion side of spiritual journey: participation and inspiration.

Participation

Believers in Jesus should never find themselves as observers when it comes to worship. To use the football analogy, they must get out of the stands and on to the field.
Worship is in many ways a heart attitude that results in tangible action. The Bible is filled with examples of God's people

actively engaged in worship. A short trip through the Psalms reinforces this.

> Sing praises to the LORD who reigns... (Ps. 9:11 NLT)
>
> Use guitars to reinforce your Hallelujahs! Play his praise on a grand piano! (Ps. 33:2 MSG)
>
> I will shout for joy and sing your praises, for you have ransomed me. (Ps. 71:23 NLT)
>
> Enter His gates with thanksgiving... (Ps. 100:4 NLT)
>
> I lift my eyes to you, O God... (Ps. 123:1 NLT)
>
> Lift up holy hands in prayer, and praise the LORD. (Ps. 134:2 NLT)
>
> ...celebrate His lovely name with music. (Ps. 135:2 NLT)
>
> I bow before your holy Temple as I worship. (Ps. 138:2 NLT)
>
> I cry out to the LORD; I plead for the LORD's mercy. (Ps. 142:1 NLT)
>
> Praise with a blast on the trumpet,
>   praise by strumming soft strings;
> Praise him with castanets and dance,
>   praise him with banjo and flute;
> Praise him with cymbals and a big bass drum,
>   praise Him with fiddles and mandolin.
>   (Ps. 150:3-5 MSG)

These instructions are not given merely to the worship leaders. They are given to the people of God. They are not given just for a worship event. They are given for worship. From these few verses I am reminded that each of us should be involved in worship. We are to be involved with our attitude and with our actions. Worship is not a passive activity for those who are followers of Christ. We engage our minds, our hearts, our souls and our strength. We search for God intently, celebrate Him fanatically, tremble before Him reverently. Sit still and remain silent before Him in awe. But worship is not just about the action of a people who have come into the presence of the Creator God. It is also about their reaction.

The Bible is filled with stories of normal men and women who had encounters with God. The imprint of God's presence forever changed the destiny of those people. Noah became a boat builder. Abram left the security of a generations old

> *No one who ever truly encountered God was ever the same afterwards.*

homeland to become the father of a landless nation. Isaac grew out of being such a mama's boy. Jacob wrestled his way out of a scheming lifestyle. Joseph changed from an arrogant, favored son to a forgiving and benevolent world leader. Moses exchanged sheep herding for people herding. Joshua went from minority voice to five star general. Gideon, an undercover wheat thresher, became a bold, Midianite thresher. Ruth went from the insecurity of a widow in her homeland of Moab to the security of family and a new home. Samuel went from intern for the priest at Shiloh to spokesperson for God. David left the pasture and moved into the throne room. Ezra the legal administrator became Ezra the inspirer. Nehemiah the food taster became a wall contractor. Matthew exchanged the tax collectors booth for homelessness. Peter, James and John gave up the fishing industry for a relatively unknown and certainly unlikely Messiah candidate. Paul surrendered position and influence for shipwrecks, beatings and hate mail.

No one who ever truly encountered God was ever the same afterwards. Yet no one completely changed overnight or without seasons with steps backwards. It was the consistent journey of a life over time that demonstrated encounters with God to be just that. The same is likely true today. An accurate evaluation of worship when we are with the family is not done with a string of stylistic questions immediately after an event. It is done over the course of weeks, months and years. It is observed in the eyes, the hearts, the voice and the lives of those who are followers of Christ. If someone who claims to be a true believer attends to worship elements in collective, community, and personal settings, yet their values are untouched, their behaviors unchanged, it seems that we can be certain of only one thing: they have not seen God and therefore have not truly worshiped.

Inspiration

Worship is not only a matter of participation for those who are the Church. It is also one of inspiration. The word inspiration as it appears in Scripture refers to the breath of God. One of Job's friends, Elihu, hesitantly entered into the dialog with Job about his predicament based on the age difference. Job was older and therefore presumed wiser than Elihu. He explained to Job that he believed that God's Spirit within people, "... the breath of the Almighty within them ..." (the inspiration of God) makes them wise and intelligent (Job 32:8 NLT). Paul writing to Timothy used the same basic word to observe that, "All Scripture is inspired by God..." (2 Tim. 3:16 NLT). Literally, Paul wrote that the words of Scripture were God breathed. If you look, you can even see Spirit in the center of the English word inspiration.

The idea of the breath of God is significant to very many passages of Scripture. In Genesis 2:7 we are told that the LORD

God created the man from the dust of the ground then breathed into him the breath of life. The Psalmist wrote, "The LORD merely spoke, and the heavens were created. He breathed the word, and all the stars were born" (Ps. 33:6 NLT). John described an event with Jesus where He recorded, "Then he breathed on them and said, 'Receive the Holy Spirit'" (Jn. 20:22 NLT). Wherever the breath of God appeared in Scripture, there was life, power and action.

Worship that is inspirational is God breathed worship; the adoration of God's people rising up to Him as a sweet smelling sacrifice of praise. As a result, He sovereignly chooses to breathe on them. They are subjected to His life and His power. In response they are driven to action, not just for the moment, but also for the future. They have met with God and will never be the same again. Put simply, they have worshiped.

WORSHIP WHILE WE ARE OUT AND ABOUT

By worship while we are out and about I am referring to the potential impact of our adoration of Jesus on the lives of people not yet faith convinced about Him. The idea has to do with whether or not the people we meet when we are scattered are persuaded that God is real and worthy of worship, based on their observations of our lives of worship. Do they see us truly see Him? Do they believe that we believe He is real? Are they compelled to consider worshiping Him because we are living a life of worship? Do our lives demonstrate a desire to worship God when we drive, with what we watch on film and television, how we spend our time, and so on? These are the kinds of things that matter regarding worship while we are out and about.

In recent years there have emerged at least two issues for the Church to consider when evaluating worship from the viewpoint of the pre-Christian person. The first is extremely foundational to everything else: Just what is the role of the still searching, pre-Christian person in regards to worship? This topic is often debated in the form of, does or can an unconvinced person really worship? There are good scholars or both sides of this question. So with nothing to lose I will add my own two cents worth to the debate. I do not think that pre-Christian, unconvinced people worship – at least not God.

The basic perspective of worship that I have tried to communicate is that worship, in order to be worship, reveals (or glorifies) God, ascribes honor to God, acknowledges and recognizes His presence, includes a response of value and life change by the worshiper. A person whose faith quest has yet to cross a line from curiously seeking unbelief to faith-convinced belief could not possibly worship in spirit and truth. They lack one key ingredient: relationship.

I do think such experimentation is very often a part of the exploration process for a seeking pre-Christian journeyer. Because of that, their presence or their involvement in an event is not in any way inappropriate. Indeed, it is likely a wonderful mile marker of the progress they are making toward a meaningful encounter with Jesus and true worship. The people of God should celebrate both their presence and their spiritual journey.

Under the inspiration of the Holy Spirit, Paul explained that God has provided His people with His Spirit so they can know the wonderful things He has for them. He went on to note that people who are not yet convinced followers of Jesus could not understand these truths because they are not possessed by

God's Spirit (1 Cor. 2:10-16). This it would seem to me must include the mysterious truths of worship.

Later in the same letter Paul acknowledged that unbelievers would likely be present at times when the Church gathered for worship. He instructed the Church to remember that eternity is in the balance whenever pre-Christians are around. He called the Church to make certain that such a person does not get the impression that you are crazy! Instead, he insisted, make your worship of God clear for them. Why? So that they will be convicted of their need for God in life and as they listen, be compelled to fall down and acknowledge that God is present. Toward that end he continued to offer some instructions regarding orderly worship for that particular congregation in light of their excesses (1 Cor. 14:22f).

> **Both our passion and the clarity of our experience will leave pre-Christian people convinced that God is among us, or convinced that He is not...**

For the Church, the Bride of Christ, to consider worship from that perspective, we must acknowledge that while unbelievers may not worship God, they are watching us when we worship God. Both our passion and the clarity of our experience will leave them convinced that God is among us, or convinced that He is not (and, subsequently, that we are crazy). Pre-Christian people do not judge those who are faith convinced followers of Jesus as a bit nutty because we stand and raise our hands or sit silently with bowed heads when we gather for worship events. What they find unacceptable is that we behave one way when we gather for worship and differently the rest of the time.

As we evaluate our worship, we must consider the observations of a watching world.

- Do they see duty or devotion?

- Do they see passion or passivity?

- Do they get it or do they want to get out?

- Do our lives reflect that we worship or does the evidence accuse us of hypocrisy?

The role of pre-Christian people in worship is more or less observation and exploration. They gather with us, they join us in the small group community, they visit with our families and they watch our lives.

This leads to the second dominating issue of our time concerning

> *What they find unacceptable is that we behave one way when we gather for worship and differently the rest of the time.*

worship from the perspective of those who are not yet convinced of our Jesus. We may safely assume that if a pre-Christian actually attends a worship gathering of the Church, then God is at work in their lives. Maybe they have met a real Christ-follower for the first time. Maybe they are watching his/her life for evidence of God. Perhaps some Kingdom ambassadors have engaged this person in spiritual conversation. Maybe the curious seeker has sought out answers to specific questions along his/her journey.

Regardless of what else is going on in their lives, they are attending gatherings of the Church where worship breaks out. At this point the Church as institution tends to ask: How do we reach out **through** our worship events? The Church, as the Bride of Christ, takes a different perspective. As the pre-Christian is drawn by the Holy Spirit to seek out the claims of Christ the question becomes: How will our Church reach out to them **in** our worship? This is the question of how seeker oriented our congregational and smaller group worship will be.

Seeker orientation became popular among evangelical churches in the western world during the latter half of the twentieth century. Dissecting theory and discussing practice has resulted in the emergence of multiple levels of seeker orientation for worship events. Some churches describe themselves as seeker driven (or seeker targeted), which leads them to create or plan their worship experiences with the seeker in mind, perhaps even for them.

These events have been compared to an evangelistic crusade rather than a worship event. Many churches that plan a seeker driven event will design a host of different experiences at other times to encourage believers in worshiping God. Early in development, the seeker driven model included limited congregational participation, a reduction in the number of Christian symbols in or on the physical plant as well as part of the actual event, secular drama with a biblically moral point, no archaic sounding language, and so on.

Other churches advance the idea of seeker friendly worship. This seems to be a middle of the road stand on the issue. These churches have a regular diet of guests attending their worship events and want to make a good first impression. They are not fully seeker directed. There will be more congregational involvement, the presence of some Christian symbols and biblical dramas. They create worship events for both believers and seekers. They are strongly influenced by an awareness of what the seeking people of their community find understandable and they attempt to incorporate those components into their corporate worship events. While not a worship event for the seeker, it is a worship event extremely aware of the seeker.

Still other churches choose what I am classifying as seeker sensitive. Like the seeker friendly congregation, there is awareness that pre-Christians are present and a desire to somehow include them in worship events. Seeker sensitive worship events are planned with the believer in mind. The strategy is to usher believers into the presence of God and allow seekers to watch. There is attention to language that communicates clearly. The concern for participation is directed toward believers and the recognition that worship is not a spectator sport. The message is: come and experience our adoration of the Groom and witness His presence among His people.

Unfortunately there are also a lot of churches that might be called seeker opposed. They intentionally choose to use something of a hidden language and mysterious symbols that are never defined, designed to communicate to the insiders only. These churches appear all over the spectrum of styles, from extreme celebration to extreme liturgical and every place in between. There is a kind of insensitivity to the presence of seekers. As with other matters of worship, the issue is not one of style, but it is one of attitude.

It seems to me a Church must wrestle with the question of how unbelievers can and should be involved in worship and the degree to which the Church (as a people) should be seeker aware. In light of my own conviction that it is important for pre-Christians to be able to observe real worship and explore its' implications for their own lives, I favor what I call a seeker sensitive worship atmosphere when the Church is gathered or in smaller group community. I think that such an

> *As with other matters of worship, the issue in seeker sensitivity is less a matter of style and more a matter of attitude.*

approach has great potential to keep the focus on God rather than on His people or the seeker. And when it comes to worship...to adoration... God is the focus.

SOME FINAL WORSHIP REMARKS

Someone has well said that worship may be the most frequently debated and least frequently experienced activity of the Church. While affirming this statement, I want to remind you that this observation is about worship, not about style. There are celebrative, praise and worship, traditional, gospel, and liturgical churches all across the land that meet each week and fail to worship God. They do not stop. They do not see Him. They do not respond to Him. They do not worship. On the other hand, there are churches across that same stylistic spectrum where people do worship God.

Since God is above style and preference, He is looking past the shape of the buildings in which we meet; beyond whether we use hymnals, songbooks, overhead cells or PowerPoint slides; deeper than how timely our transitions are; further than the rhythm or scholasticism of points in sermons or lessons; and past the professional quality of the choir, instrumentalist, or praise team/band. As Samuel learned long ago, "The LORD doesn't see things the way you see them. People judge by outward appearance, but the LORD looks at the heart" (1 Sam. 16:7 NLT). God is looking past our actions to see our intentions. Since our worship is to be directed toward God, we must embrace worship as He sees it or we will forever be destined to evaluate worship meaninglessly.

Worship is therefore the natural response of God's people when they see Him. Because it is a natural response, the content of worship (God) is far more important than the style in which we worship. I will always think of Adele every time I hear the Carpenter's song, "The Top of the World." That was the song getting air time on the radio when we grew to know that we loved each other. In much the same way, moments with God are attached to things like music in our spiritual journey. Worship leads to wonderful traditions. Take caution: **When maintaining a tradition is as important as encountering God then the tradition has become traditionalism, which is idolatry.**

Worship is never a reverent laced effort to call God down out of His heaven to meet with us. Neither is it an exhausting effort to jump up to Him. Instead, worship is stopping and recognizing Him right now. It is seeing Him, acknowledging Him and responding to Him.

I once heard a pastor describing a day of medical tests that he had endured. To hear him talk, it was an extensive array of exams that lasted better than eight grueling hours. He said that one thing he couldn't help but notice was that no matter what test he was engaged in, he was always attached to a heart monitor. If he was on the treadmill, he was wired. If he was sitting on an exam table, he was wired. If he walked stairs, he was wired. If he endured uncomfortable positions on the x-ray table, he was wired. If he laid back to rest, he was wired. They monitored his heart under stress and in rest. At the close of the day he had an interview with the tending physician. He talked with the doctor about the whole day, but asked specifically, Why all the tests on the heart? The doctor made this observation, "We know that if your heart is good we can address anything else that might show up in your health." Worship is that beating heart of the Bride of Christ, plain and simple. It is the natural function of the Church. If the heart is good, you can address anything else.

CONCLUSIONS

The day finally came for Selah. The home was completed. Selah had readied herself for this moment. She had done the hard work of carving out a new identity – she had embraced a new way of doing things, a new family to encourage and strengthen her, a new level of hope and expectations for friendships. She made decisions differently now. And she adored Justus... not just like, not even just love, but really adored him.

Her life was forever changed. It was both an immediate change (being) and a process of change (becoming). But it was change... real change. She was leaving one way of being and clinging to a new way. Her betrothal season was a time for her to become who she really was.

Though it felt like forever since the covenant was announced, since betrothal began – now everything was happening so quickly – expected, yet so surprising – dreamed of, yet more wonderful. The march through the streets, the singing and dancing echoing through the otherwise quiet countryside, the lamps igniting the otherwise dark landscape – everything was exciting. As surely as she thought she would never forget the beginning of this journey, she knew she would never forget this moment.

But, what if Selah had squandered – wasted her time? What if she had decided to do nothing during the betrothal? What if she had opted to just tie a knot and hang on? Justus would surely have still come. It was his very nature to keep his word. He loved her dearly and thoroughly. But what he would have found would have been... disappointing. And the last thing Selah wanted to do was disappoint him.

My dream in this venture has been to challenge you to think of Church as a *who* rather than a *what*. Specifically, to think of your Church as a Bride whose Groom has worked tirelessly to prepare a perfect home for her and who is returning to carry her to that home.

- A Groom whose identity is one she will move heaven and earth to adopt

- A Groom who invites her by a compelling example to a new way of living – not enslavement, but living as a servant of a higher calling... a greater mission... surrendering her dreams to His

- A Groom who ups the ante on what deep, transformational friendship is really like and how a safe family environment empowers radical life

- A Groom whose example is so otherly... so holy... that she cannot help but voluntarily change the way she makes decisions, adopting new values and seeing life in completely otherly ways

- A Groom whose love is so real – so present – so breathtaking that each time she sees Him she melts in His arms. One for whom the only phrase that even approaches capturing the depth of her love is adoring worship

I hope that your mind has meandered through the life of your own Church as you have read each page. I pray that you have wrestled with every issue raised and honestly begun to consider where you and your Church are right now. My guess is that you have seen areas where there are strengths to celebrate and places where you could give a little attention.

I suppose one of the things that I have feared most through this project is that someone might walk away from the read discouraged. They might look at their own Church, in light of these ponderings, shrug their shoulders and reason, "Oh well… we'll never be like that." But you will. Really! In a beautiful section of Holy Spirit's letter to the churches in Ephesus, Paul uses the example of an exemplary marriage to help his readers see this vision of Christ, the Groom and Church, the Bride. Along that way he reminds them:

> …Christ loved the church. He gave up his life for her to make her holy and clean… He did this to present her to himself as a glorious church without a spot or wrinkle or any other blemish. Instead, she will be holy and without fault. (Eph. 5:25-27 NLT)

I hope you see that '*will be*'. I know He is talking about The Church rather than just your Church or my Church. But our churches are part of *The Church*, are they not? This means among other things, there is hope for us yet.

There is no such thing as a perfect local Church in the here and now. A former professor of mine once advised, "Millwood, if you ever find a perfect Church, whatever you do, do not join it, for you will surely mess things up for them." Perfec_tion_ is really not the issue here. Perfec_ting_, now that's another matter altogether.

Most of my life I have done Church by model, by imitation, and/or by program. The model of some Church, considered successful by the standards I had come to believe; or the imitation of some highly visible leader that I admired; or the latest and greatest program sent to me by my denomination. Because of such a pattern, I have jumped from this program to that, from this model to the next model, and from leader to leader.

In a fit of frustration some years back, I began a journey to ask a different question: Just what is it to **be** Church? This book represents a point on that journey. It is what the LORD is teaching me so far.

Early on I confessed to you some level of frustration with the Church – the Bride of Christ. That frustration was fuel for this journey.

I still get frustrated with churches – but for wholly different reasons now. Along this way I am learning to see her real beauty – the hopes her Groom holds for her – the price the Father determined to pay for her, and I get frustrated that so many local expressions of the Church do not see it. It's as if she stands in front of a mirror, but instead of seeing herself as He sees her, she just sees the temporary blemishes and then mind-numbingly accepts them as inevitable... just the way things are. *That* breaks my heart.

The descriptions throughout this book have been intended to paint a new portrait of her. It is a portrait of a local Church on the road toward health. It is a portrait of a Bride who determines to apply herself to the betrothal season – to play her part in the forging of this new family. And she is beautiful... both as she is (remember, Justus fell in love with Selah as she was), *and* as she one day will be! Such a Church can exist. Here is what she looks like:

- The people who are the Church live with a conscious awareness that Jesus is here... now... on mission, and they are constantly stopping their agendas in order to actually see Him. Whenever they catch a glimpse of their adored Groom, they **worship** Him. They just can't help themselves.

- At least one reason they see Him is because they are **listening to His Voice and submitting to His authority**. It is all about His mission, His vision, His values, His mission field. They consciously put their missions under His mission. They work tirelessly to keep that order to things. Because they are about the same things that He is about, they just seem to see Him with greater frequency than others.

- Being fully submitted to Him, they rally around one common unity. Their own diversity or interests no longer distract them. That common unity is the Groom, Jesus. He is the One who holds them together. He is the source of their shared **community**. He is the One who provides relationship with the Father and mission to the world.

- In their local expressions **everyone serves** in natural ways along this journey. As they serve, God's Spirit empowers good hearts and hands in such a way that their acts of service end up affecting each other as well as those around them not yet reached by this Good News.

- As they serve like this they demonstrate that they are indeed **disciples of Jesus** becoming more and more like Him. So much so that others around them recognize the increasingly unmistakable image of the Master in them.

They fix their eyes on Jesus, wrap their arms around each other, and live on His mission field with all the enthusiasm and persistence of the very first Church.

The Good News Bible translates Ecclesiastes 7:29 as follows:

This is all I have learned: God made us plain and simple but we have made ourselves very complicated!

That little verse captures something of the essence of the message of this book. God's design for the Church – a Bride for His Son – is really plain and simple. Years of tinkering with His plan have too often resulted in complex organizational structures and complicated policies and procedures… exhausting. We are the ones who complicated things. He is the One who made us plain and simple.

So, I join a quiet chorus who would call us back to the simple life of Jesus – a Groom who has gone to prepare a place for His Bride – a Groom who will come again to receive her for Himself – a Groom who loves us so dearly and thoroughly that we do not want to disappoint Him. Let's change the way that we see Church… the way that we live Church. **Let us love and cherish Him from this day, forward.**

PEOPLE I'VE LEARNED FROM AND YOU CAN TOO

In the *Acknowledgement* page I confessed I'm a *mutt*. Nowhere in my life is that more true than when it comes to the books I've read. Over the course of time spent wrestling with the topics in this book alone, I've read tons of books from loads of authors.

It would be impossible to list them all. So I have picked out a representative sampling. I started to categorize them by the sections of the book, but the truth is all of them are *both* broader *and* more focused than the categorizations would allow.

So I offer these as a means of encouraging you to keep on learning about life as the Bride of Christ.

Just one warning: the temptation to *settle* for a lifetime of book learning rather than learning by life experience is significant in our age of resources *ad infinitum*. Be selective. Read deeply. *Apply* liberally.

A Long Obedience in the Same Direction, Eugene Peterson
A Work of Heart, Reggie McNeal
Blue Like Jazz, Donald Miller
Church Without Walls, Jim Petersen
Community 101, Gilbert Bilezikian
Everybody's Normal Till You Get To Know Them, John Ortberg
Experiencing God, Henry Blackaby and Claude King
Freedom of Simplicity, Richard Foster
Growing True Disciples, George Barna
Hearing God, Developing a Conversational Relationship with God, Dallas Willard

Holy Discontent, Bill Hybels
Holy Rewired, David Phillips
Jesus on Leadership, C. Gene Wilkes
Lead Like Jesus, Lessons from the Greatest Leadership Role Model of All Time, Ken Blanchard and Phil Hodges
Live Sent, you are a letter, Jason Dukes
Living Proof, Jim Petersen
Making Room for Life, Randy Frazee
Messy Spirituality, Michael Yaconelli
More Ready Than You Realize, Brian McLaren
Natural Church Development, Christian Schwarz
Pouring New Wine into Old Wineskins, Aubrey Malphurs
Practicing Greatness: 7 Disciplines of Extraordinary Spiritual Leaders, Reggie McNeal
Rediscovering Church, Lynn and Bill Hybels
Reframing Spiritual Formation, Edward Hammett
Revolution in Leadership, Reggie McNeal
Strengthening the Soul of your Leadership, Ruth Haley Barton
The Art of Personal Evangelism, Will McRaney
The Celtic Way of Evangelism, George Hunter
The Character of Leadership, Jeff Iorg
The Cost of Discipleship, Dietrich Bonhoeffer
The Disciple Making Church, Bill Hull
The Life You've Always Wanted, John Ortberg
The Overload Syndrome, Richard Swenson
The Purpose Driven Church, Rick Warren
The Ragamuffin Gospel, Brennan Manning
The Safest Place on Earth, Larry Crabb
The Starfish and the Spider, Ori Brafman and Rod Beckstrom
The Walk, Gene Getz

Transforming Discipleship, Greg Ogden
Transitioning, Leading Your Church Through Change, Dan Southerland
Upside Down, The Paradox of Servant Leadership, Stacy Rinehart
Worship Evangelism, Sally Morgenthaler

CONNECT

If you have any interest in continuing to think and talk about the health of the Bride, here are a few ways that you can join me in that journey...

facebook.com/simplymillwood

simplymillwood.wordpress.com

twitter.com/simplymillwood

I'll see you around!

ABOUT THE AUTHOR

Hi. Thanks for purchasing (or at least picking up and thumbing through) *To Love and To Cherish From This Day Forward*. I am so honored that you would do so. Let me introduce myself. My name is Randy.

I've been following Jesus for a little over 40 years now – sometimes close and, sadly, sometimes at a distance – my fault – never His.

I am married to my high school sweetheart who is my best friend in the world. Our marriage has not been without plenty of trial and error (again, my fault), but we are making it, with great joy! We have two adult sons who we love and are so incredibly proud of. Those *little boys* of ours have families of their own now making us grandparents!! [Just ask; we'll be glad to show you the pictures.]

Adele and I are also the full-time administrative managers for a spoiled rotten Pembroke Welsh Corgi.

We remain a part of one Church (Horizon Church) while exploring a new House Church Network with some similarly minded soul friends

I really believe there are only 2 seasons in a year: baseball and Christmas. There are always Christmas reminders up in our home until the pitchers/catchers report for spring training, and they come right back out after the last pitch of the World Series.

I have served in some form of ministry for decades including about every Church role you can imagine from founding pastor to bus pastor and everything in between. I never, ever wanted to work for a denominational entity and have now worked for several for a couple of decades.

I have too much education... I used to kid with my mom that "her son is a doctor and can't even prescribe aspirin!"

I am sort of a freelance Christian worker. The main way God provides for us is through my full-time work with the churches of the Baptist Convention of Maryland/Delaware where I coach pastoral leaders, particularly the soul care of pastors and pastoral staff; consult with small, home/market-based groups; and champion relational spiritual formation. Additionally, I play a variety of roles with Doctor of Ministry students from various institutions. Finally, I am a member of the Academic Council and faculty of a completely online, purpose-driven seminary called Rockbridge Seminary.

I love simple, organic expressions of *Church*, and smaller, life-transforming groups.

Made in the USA
Charleston, SC
10 March 2013